When
mc
meets
DOG

... it leads to a unique friendship; one that can change men's lives

What a difference a dog makes!

Chris Blazina PhD

Hubble & Hattie

The Hubble & Hattie imprint was launched in 2009 and is named in memory of two very special Westie sisters who lived with Veloce's proprietors. Since the first book, many more have been added to the list, all with the same underlying objective: to be of real benefit to the species they cover, at the same time promoting compassion, understanding and respect between all animals (including human ones!) All Hubble & Hattie publications offer ethical, high quality content and presentation, plus great value for money.

More books from Hubble & Hattie –

Among the Wolves: Memoirs of a wolf handler (Shelbourne)

Animal Grief: How animals mourn (Alderton)

Babies, kids and dogs – creating a safe and harmonious relationship (Fallon & Davenport)

Because this is our home ... the story of a cat's progress (Bowes)

Camper vans, ex-pats & Spanish Hounds: from road trip to rescue – the strays of Spain (Coates & Morris)

Cat Speak: recognising & understanding behaviour (Rauth-Widmann)

Charlie – The dog who came in from the wild (Tenzin-Dolma)

Clever dog! Life lessons from the world's most successful animal (O'Meara)

Complete Dog Massage Manual, The – Gentle Dog Care (Robertson)

Dieting with my dog: one busy life, two full figures ... and unconditional love (Frezon)

Dinner with Rover: delicious, nutritious meals for you and your dog to share (Paton-Ayre)

Dog Cookies: healthy, allergen-free treat recipes for your dog (Schöps)

Dog-friendly Gardening: creating a safe haven for you and your dog (Bush)

Dog Games – stimulating play to entertain your dog and you (Blenski)

Dog Relax – relaxed dogs, relaxed owners (Pilguj)

Dog Speak: recognising & understanding behaviour (Blenski)

Dogs on Wheels: travelling with your canine companion (Mort)

Emergency First Aid for dogs: at home and away Revised Edition (Bucksch)

Exercising your puppy: a gentle & natural approach – Gentle Dog Care (Robertson & Pope)

Fun and Games for Cats (Seidl)

Gods, ghosts, and black dogs – the fascinating folklore and mythology of dogs (Coren)

Helping minds meet – skills for a better life with your dog (Zulch & Mills)

Home alone and happy – essential life skills for preventing separation anxiety in dogs and puppies (Mallatratt)

Know Your Dog – The guide to a beautiful relationship (Birmelin)

Life skills for puppies – laying the foundation of a loving, lasting relationship (Zuch & Mills)

Living with an Older Dog – Gentle Dog Care (Alderton & Hall)

Miaow! Cats really are nicer than people! (Moore)

My cat has arthritis – but lives life to the full! (Carrick)

My dog has arthritis – but lives life to the full! (Carrick)

My dog has cruciate ligament injury – but lives life to the full! (Haüsler & Friedrich)

My dog has epilepsy – but lives life to the full! (Carrick)

My dog has hip dysplasia – but lives life to the full! (Haüsler & Friedrich)

My dog is blind – but lives life to the full! (Horsky)

My dog is deaf – but lives life to the full! (Willms)

My Dog, my Friend: heart-warming tales of canine companionship from celebrities and other extraordinary people (Gordon)

No walks? No worries! Maintaining wellbeing in dogs on restricted exercise (Ryan & Zulch)

Partners – Everyday working dogs being heroes every day (Walton)

Smellorama – nose games for dogs (Theby)

Swim to recovery: canine hydrotherapy healing – Gentle Dog Care (Wong)

A tale of two horses – a passion for free will teaching (Gregory)

Tara – the terrier who sailed around the world (Forrester)

The Truth about Wolves and Dogs: dispelling the myths of dog training (Shelbourne)

Waggy Tails & Wheelchairs (Epp)

Walking the dog: motorway walks for drivers & dogs revised edition (Rees)

When man meets dog – what a difference a dog makes (Blazina)

Winston ... the dog who changed my life (Klute)

The quite very actual adventures of Worzel Wooface (Pickles)

You and Your Border Terrier – The Essential Guide (Alderton)

You and Your Cockapoo – The Essential Guide (Alderton)

Your dog and you – understanding the canine psyche (Garratt)

For post publication news, updates and amendments relating to this book please visit www.hubbleandhattie.com/extras/ HH4879

Illustrations courtesy of Laura Baisden.

www.hubbleandhattie.com

First published April 2016 by Veloce Publishing Limited, Veloce House, Parkway Farm Business Park, Middle Farm Way, Poundbury, Dorchester, Dorset, DT1 3AR, England. Fax 01305 250479/email info@hubbleandhattie.com/web www.hubbleandhattie.com. ISBN: 978-1-845848-79-8 UPC: 6-36847-04879-2 © Chris Blazina & Veloce Publishing Ltd 2016. All rights reserved. With the exception of quoting brief passages for the purpose of review, no part of this publication may be recorded, reproduced or transmitted by any means, including photocopying, without the written permission of Veloce Publishing Ltd. Throughout this book logos, model names and designations, etc, have been used for the purposes of identification, illustration and decoration. Such names are the property of the trademark holder as this is not an official publication.

Readers with ideas for books about animals, or animal-related topics, are invited to write to the editorial director of Veloce Publishing at the above address. British Library Cataloguing in Publication Data – A catalogue record for this book is available from the British Library. Typesetting, design and page make-up all by Veloce Publishing Ltd on Apple Mac. Printed in India by Replika Press.

Contents

"When the Man waked up he said,

'What is Wild Dog doing here?'

And the Woman said,

"His name is not Wild Dog any more,

but the First Friend,

because he will be our friend

for always and always and always.'"

Rudyard Kipling

Foreword

Our relationship with our companion animals – especially our dogs – is very important, and, for many, one of the most influential in our lives, which often shapes our appreciation of love, or at least our ability to know affection and commitment to another. But we must accept that a dog has a shorter lifespan than do we, usually just ten to fourteen years, which is only a small part of our lives, meaning that we may have many companion dogs. What is novel in *When man meets dog* is the appreciation that the bond between us and our dogs does not end at the time of their death.

There are many books and popular articles that recount the dog-human relationship, especially from the female perspective. This may not be surprising, as dogs are often viewed as not only members of the family, but juvenile members – children, that is – and women are the recognized child caretakers and leaders of the family pack. Of course, men have a long-time record as fathers, but this is not often appreciated in connection with the canine family member: the generalization is that a man is more disciplined in function and emotion in the dog-human bond. To be sure, the assertion that a dog is 'man's best friend' is well known, and emphasizes the animal's role and importance to us, more so than the other way around. As a general rule, in scholarly and popular literature, the male point of view is less explored.

Dr Blazina observes that a man with a dog can be alone with others: that is, be alone without being lonely. Such solitude encourages the man to explore thoughts and feelings not possible whilst with other people, who almost always have to comment, judge, or otherwise communicate in some fashion. Men are often challenged when dealing with high impact emotional areas such as affection, and, as a general rule, in our culture, men are more inhibited about openly dealing with matters of emotional impact, be these good *or* bad.

Psychiatrist Aaron Katcher noted that men are far less likely than women to show affectionate touch in public, although used touch to comfort their companion animals in veterinary waiting rooms as much as women did – perhaps the only situation where this occurs. The most logical reason for this is that our animals do not carry with them any of the baggage usually associated with people, as age, gender, or ethnicity are not taken into account or do not apply, and the animals never offer personal judgment.

In addition to affection, men have special difficulty in expressing and dealing with the sadness associated with the death of a loved one, and it is important that they learn how to understand and cope with these feelings of loss.

This book provides an honest introspective of man's feelings about his relationship with a beloved dog, especially at the time of the animal's death, which is actually only a small part of the total time spent together and enjoyed by both, which can extend beyond the boundaries of life. It may even, in some cases, extend our lives. The book explores just such an important period in the author's life, and perhaps in many other of us.

Dr Blazina notes that writing his book was a therapeutic experience for him, as he better understands the loss of his beloved dog, Kelsey. I have no doubt that readers of the book will also derive great therapeutic value, too.

Alan M Beck
Dorothy N McAllister
Professor of Animal Ecology
College of Veterinary Medicine
Purdue University
West Lafayette, Indiana

1

The story of the bond
– when man meets
dog

"It is true that those we meet can change us, sometimes so profoundly
that we are not the same afterwards, even unto our names.
"Doesn't the telling of something always become a story?"
– Yann Martel, *Life of Pi*

Ever since I was a little boy, stories have been the way I have tried to understand the complexities of life. They sustained my attention even in the most challenging of circumstances. This included sitting on the hard, wooden pews of our church for what seemed like an eternity. My mind usually wandered, and eventually I would nod off to sleep. My inattentiveness and napping during the service caused my mother a great deal of consternation, and apparently it did not sit well with God, either: at least that is what my mom told me. So, out of a sense of desperation or resignation, I sometimes really tried to listen.

Luckily, there was the occasional good storyteller in the pulpit, who shared a vivid account about someone to illustrate a point, and even if that person was long dead or you never met them, it felt like it might be worth sitting still for a few minutes to hear what they were about. If I liked what I was hearing well enough, it might linger in my thoughts for a while. If it was especially compelling, maybe I learned something about how to be a good person, or a better way to treat my fellow man, often without knowing it.

While it happened in a different context, the subtle art of storytelling was at its best when used by my animal companions. They were the best communicators of all, in part because of the ways they conveyed a message without words. The lessons to be learned were embedded within our interactions, incorporated at a visceral level. Their tutoring style was neither contrived nor forced. It just involved a simple beauty and eloquence that sustained my attention for more than fourteen years at a time. They told me the story of what it meant to connect with someone at the deepest level. Our interactions impacted on me through the relationship that was created: something I will refer to as the 'bond' we shared.

Animals have shaped my life. Some of my best recollections include them. Even as a young boy, I was drawn to their company. When our little house, filled with ten or more people, felt particularly cramped, I would take a seat on the back steps and talk things over with our gentle German Shepherd. I remember him sitting very still, alert and attentive, almost like he was on point, but with a much calmer demeanor. As I recounted the events of what had just happened on the other side of the brick wall, he would occasionally glance in my direction. As I talked and eventually felt some release, I would pet him as a token of thanks. We would then go play. These exchanges influenced my aspirations for how I thought a good listener, and then a psychologist, should be. A calming, steady presence can make an impression. I have even unwittingly adopted a similar demeanor in my counseling work: a catch-and-release style of looking and then glancing away.

Besides being used as a means to hold my attention during church services as a boy, stories are also a place to temporarily store unfinished business. While it is good to hear about someone else's entire tale, most of us do not fully work through all our own experiences. We are often not even aware of making life-changing choices in the moment: ones whose significance is only fully realized later, in hindsight. Though I have imagined at times what it would be like to have an all-knowing narrator following me around, one who sounds a lot like Morgan Freeman, saying things like, "Well, that was when Chris made the decision he would later come to regret ..." If I had that going for me, I might have the foresight to straighten things out. Short of this, living our own stories is more like a book you may be reading or writing. It is accomplished line-by-line, chapter-by-chapter; not always sure about how it will end.

However, the significant chapters of our lives can be revisited, taking what feels raw and unprocessed, sorting it through a little at a time with each new immersion. Every telling allows the storyline to become clearer, with distinct themes emerging that provide insight about where each of us comes from, and where we are headed. Ultimately, personal stories are told for our own transformation, ushering transition, loss, and personal pain into a more settled place.

The approach to storytelling I am describing is especially important when curious friends ask us to tell them what happened in our latest quest for a relationship. Why it did not work out, or, for that matter, why they *never* do. Or could we please elaborate more about the origins of our dysfunctional family? None of these topics is as easily accessed as pulling a book from a shelf, which contains a detailed glossary or table of contents. Instead, in these moments, the sought-after words are elusive, not even coming close to yielding a full understanding of our experience, and our associates may scratch their heads in response, struggling to comprehend the meaning.

It is at this juncture that many – myself included – resort to telling a story. We can frustrate our listener with a dry and obscure explanation, but they can eagerly drink in an account that starts, 'Once upon a time …' The challenge of finding words for difficult or indescribable topics can be overcome by relaying parts of our experience in narrative form. Stories do not have to be deconstructed fully in order to carry meaning.

I can say with certainty that the most complex story I have ever tried to comprehend involves the reasons my animal companions have meant so much to me. Why the presence of a shelter dog named Kelsey, and another one called Sadie, have changed the direction of my life. This book details my journey, prompted by the loss of one old friend, and the ways the other still helps me to grow and heal. Each continues to teach me lessons that I am not always aware I am learning. What a difference a dog makes.

Stories have a beginning, a middle, and an end

The Greek philosopher Aristotle suggested that all stories have a beginning, a middle, and an end.[1] By utilizing Aristotle's formula, an excursion is undertaken. Our quiet and safe beginnings give way to an adventure that builds toward the middle part of the tale, only finding resolution by working it through to the conclusion. Everyone knows leaving at intermission will result in frustration and loss. Only in the final act can one find satisfaction. Psychologically speaking, the three-part story is both enlivening and comforting. It gives the feeling of having lived on the razor's edge, wrestling with life's challenges, while also providing the sense of mastery over the current problem, and the courage to face those like it still to come. Aristotle's approach to storytelling can be applied to many great storylines, including how an animal companion figures prominently in our lives.

A few years ago, my barber, Rick, and I were talking about my early work on *When man meets dog*. Being a like-minded dog person, he said that it sounded interesting, but he would never read it. He went on to say, "All those books finish the same way: the dog always dies at the end."

Rick's perceptive comments rang a bell. I did not want to write a book about sad endings that did not also carry with it the possibility of hope. However, the hope had to be real; not something I made up to buffer the reality of grief. It took years for me to fully comprehend, but loss is actually not the end of our stories. It is, instead, the subject of the second act.

The third and, perhaps, most important part of our story involves what comes next, which I will refer to as 'forming a continuing bond with those we have lost.' This is a way of having a permanent connection with those who are important, even after they are gone. Most of us have to look at the story with fresh eyes in order to restructure our tale: one that has the potential power of becoming a living legacy, rendering comfort and a sense of connection.[2]

Our updated story rightfully begins with chapters highlighting attachment, how our bond forms, and the ways in which it impacts our lives. This part of the tale can have many twists and turns, contributing to the meaning of our relationship. It can involve the circumstances of our first meeting, and, for most, how a pet is transformed into an animal companion – by definition a close friend or family member. This reflects the sentiment of a significant percentage of Americans who have dogs and cats as a part of their household.[3] Because I am one of those people, I use 'animal companion' rather than 'pet' in my writing.

A key theme throughout this story is how the bond can literally reshape our notion of relationships. Some of the things learned may involve giving in ways never before thought possible, or, on the flipside, receiving the unique gift of support during difficult life changes. Regardless of the exact circumstances, the presence of an animal companion can, at the deepest level, provide the hope that at least one meaningful connection can be made; perhaps laying the foundation for many others. I have come to believe that the meaning of the bond has certain universal qualities, but that it also has a unique significance in tune with the occurrences that affect each individual's life. This is one of the reasons I have to share the backdrop of my own life, otherwise, the bond's true significance for me can never really be known.

The middle part of our story details loss. Research on grieving the loss of an animal companion shows that it reflects one's level of attachment. The loss can be experienced in various ways, such as sadness, a preoccupation with an animal companion, physical sensations like a lump in the throat, and even through trying to reunite in our nightly dreams.[3] The most intense part of the bereavement period can, on average, last between six and twelve months, but grief can be experienced for years. While that is more of a clinical account of what happens, what is most important is how the loss affects us.

Some grief experts focus on what is referred to as post-traumatic growth – the possibility of positive psychological change as a result of struggling with challenging life circumstances.[4] The resulting transformation represents potential shifts in an individual's way of understanding the world. It involves more than simply immersing ourselves back into the same personal narrative after a period of sadness' instead, there is a change in us at a fundamental level: becoming a little wiser, more open, and perhaps perceiving our own story and the stories of others in different ways. If our animal companions take on unique importance, part of the challenge lies in putting the meaning of that bond in its rightful place within our lives when it is time to grieve. Some discover that their animal companion took over for other lost loved ones from the formative years. On the other hand, the bond with a canine friend might be unique among all relationships, both old and new. For many, recounting our own story changes who we are. I know it did for me.

Our bonds with our animal companions last, on average, twelve to fourteen years. Most humans live much longer, and a permanent way to preserve the importance of our relationship is necessary. The last part of the story focuses on the 'continuing bond,' which recognizes that the loss is real, while also attempting to find a new way of maintaining the connection with an old friend who has passed away.[5] This type of bond is a testament to our relationship; an inspiration that rightfully continues to impact our lives. The newly revised third act of our play allows for a different and more meaningful conclusion, one that keeps us connected to all that has been experienced.

There are many ways to find this new type of bond. It can happen, as mentioned above, through post-traumatic growth. There is also the option of finding meaning in the loss, such as fighting for cures to diseases, in the form of social activism for animal rights, or fostering shelter dogs. Some choose to create a memorial – naming a kennel after a lost animal companion – or honoring their memory through plaster paw prints. Rituals can also be enacted when special anniversaries come to mind, and are subsequently celebrated. Some form a continued bond by being part of a community where stories are shared in person, on the internet, or in the privacy of one's home. The new bond can even exist by calling on a memory of an animal companion to provide support and guidance.

About twelve years ago, when I lost Kelsey, I started writing down what I could remember about our adventures. I did not realize at the time that I was also simultaneously trying to create a continuing bond. Along with this came an understanding about all of the different roles she played in my life. I discovered that our bond had many complex layers, which changed over time. My personal accounts are not about jaw-dropping adventures of climbing the Himalayas together, or going on search-and-rescue missions, but simpler kinds of tales. Tales that involve the everyday part of living and loving, and, sadly, at some point, the loss of someone close to me. Some of the details are blurry from the passage of time. In some ways, they may come across as being similar to a parable or tall tale. However, any embellishment is unintended, and pales in comparison to the undeniable truth that Kelsey changed my life. As I reflect, I try to decipher exactly how this came to be. Some of it was not evident to me at the time, and other things I have only found words for now that she is gone.

My story got stuck in the second part of the play – loss – for many years. I thought that was all there was. A place so unsatisfying and frustrating that I began marshaling my forces in various ways in order to overcome it. My work as a psychologist, researcher, and professor helped, but, as I said before, this is not an academic book. Originally, I wanted it to be one. That way, I could hide behind ideas and thoughts, camouflaging another important aspect of this story, the struggles of what it means to be a man.

Men

I have spent my career focusing on the psychology of men, which essentially involves the culturally conditioned ways males are taught to think, feel, and act. Even now, I do not pretend that these ideas do not have direct relevance for me in my life. I am just reluctant to admit it, write about it, and allow others to take a closer look at my own limitations.

The decision to do so is not a masochistic one, but rather a topic important enough to go against the grain of what I have been taught since I was a boy. The messages include how maleness is synonymous with embracing isolation and inaccessibility, and donning a culturally prescribed persona. I have been educated to anticipate my audience and act accordingly. This involves saying less than I feel on occasions that seem too risky, or when revealing too much is at odds with what I have been trained about how men carry themselves.

Other fall-out includes failing to successfully acquire some of the skills needed to recognize what goes on inside my own inner world, and that of others. There is a lot of uncertainty, clutter, and confusion in striving to be 'man enough.' While male socialization provides its own unique set of pitfalls and drawbacks, men like me are not from another planet. Instead, many of us are taught to approach masculinity as a performance art that seems strange, confusing, and even alien to others. Needless to say, these issues are at the heart of the story that affects success and failure in relationships.

Another detail to consider is how much the story I share is an everyman tale, one that most males will resonate with. There are some nuances to reflect on before deciding if it meets the terms for universal agreement, the first being that I am middle-aged. I go to a local coffee shop, and a teenager who identifies himself as my 'barista' refers to me as 'Bud,' 'Buddy,' and 'Bro,' all within the span of the few minutes that we interact. I do not relate to what seems to be a misplaced attempt at male egalitarianism. In fact, I am initially too shocked to even comment, and just walk away with my cup of joe. I would never have thought to talk that way to someone so much older when I was that young, as it was seen as a sign of disrespect.

Respect was something that was earned in the working class world I grew up in: a commodity as precious as personal honor and loyalty. None of these things was so easily handed over a counter as a styrofoam cup. But, then again, I come back to the heart of the problem with masculinity, or at least the version I know ... There are all of these rules to be learned, some of which easily become rigid, and lack a situation-specific flexibility: these are the ones that, in the heat of the moment, make it difficult to have perspective.

The current generation of younger men faces a number of cultural issues, not all of which are completely foreign to me. Sociologist Michael Kimmel, author of *Guyland: The Perilous World Where Boys Become Men*, spells out the challenges that accompany being a twenty-something male, and sustaining relationships even under the best circumstances.[6]

Making things worse is a prolonged period of adolescence, and the growing educational and earning discrepancies between men and women. Women who make more money and are better educated are less likely to settle for men in danger of being set adrift, still living in their parents' basement at the age of thirty.

And yet, relationship concerns and ego bruising are not the exclusive realm of twenty-somethings. The recent recession has also taken on definitive characteristics of the He-cession.[7] By some estimates, 82 percent of the job losses experienced have befallen men, and, of these, baby boomers are especially concerned about their pensions and retirement accounts. While the vast majority of boomers marry at some point, being in a relationship is not the same as flourishing in one. The National Center for Family & Marriage Research shows that, despite the overall divorce rate in the US dropping over the last 20 years, it has doubled for people age 50 and over.[8] This phenomenon is known as the 'grey divorce.' The culmination of new cultural developments are laid on top of the already existing ill-effects, making relationships seem even more daunting for men.

Work and love may not be what they were for Marlboro Man, and he is in an unfamiliar place of vulnerability as a result. Chances are that he is not the one riding off into the sunset this time, but his job and significant other who are saying 'goodbye' instead. There are distinct underlining themes which are, in large part, responsible for the current troubles of men, each of which has received more than thirty-five years of research by psychologists such as Dr James O'Neil.[9] O'Neil's work supports the notion that men's conflicts about masculinity are causing significant difficulty, leading to increases of depression, anxiety, and interpersonal problems.

These conflicts are the by-products of lopsided traditional male norms: the rules and guidelines for how men enact masculinity in America, and include skewed notions about success, power, and competition. Men rate their entire worth and failure by acquired material success. If a man cannot measure up, or is unable to better the previous generation's level of prosperity, then mark him as a disappointment.

Men not only struggle to make real ties with romantic significant others, but to make male friends as well. Males are blocked from utilizing a previously longstanding American tradition emphasizing bonds of brotherhood, replaced instead with misgivings about homophobia and competition for limited resources. There is also the struggle for young and middle-aged men to balance the strains of work and family demands. In the world of changing gender roles, males struggle with retaining their sense of masculinity, while also discovering new ways of being a connected father and husband.

Finally, the biggest and most consistent problem is that of a restricted emotional range and fluency. Men do not learn the skillsets that enable deep ties to be formed, which also affects their ability to grieve when significant losses eventually occur: the loss of friends, family, and, of course, animal companions.

Michael Kimmel estimates that upwards of 70 percent of American men endorse some version of the traditional male norms.[10] It would be an understatement to say that the way males enact this brand of masculinity impacts their lives. I use the term 'we' from time to time throughout the book as an attempt to underscore some of the more widespread experiences, which transcend age, social status, and other contextual descriptors. As men, we face some challenges ...

One of the solutions to the problems brought on by male socialization may, at first, seem like an unscientific one. Sharing my thoughts with certain colleagues seems to strain their understanding and my credibility, unless, that is, they know something about the theme to which I was referring – the bond between man and dog. Researchers and clinicians from around the world study the importance of human-animal interaction. While not a cure-all, the connection with animal companions has a growing list of research-supported effects on the psychological and social well-being of those who enjoy their company,[11] ranging from lowering blood pressure to the social benefits the bond brings.

The bond's power even seems to benefit the so-called solitary man I describe in this book: he who resides on a metaphoric island, far from the reach of others, seemingly self-sufficient; foreswearing most, if not all, of his need for others. I am reluctant to admit that this description is, in some ways, a depiction of me. At the same time, a small part of my brain fires up with, "Good job! Continue on your way to achieving a manly isolated status." Regardless, even an overly self-contained and withdrawn man may become more accessible in the presence of the bond.

There are more than 83 million dogs in households throughout the United States.[12] One study found that 41 percent of men rate their animal companions as just as affectionate, if not more so, than their significant other.[13] This does not imply that human friends and partners are doing something wrong, only that, clearly, there is something distinctive in the tie between man and dog that is worth knowing more about. Sometimes, the most revealing discoveries occur when examining a life in transition or under duress, as this provides an unfettered look at the inner workings of men's psyches, and, with it, our perception of the bond. Perhaps a window into my world as a middle-aged male working through the remnants of change not only reveals what came *before* in my life, and how this shaped me, but also, more importantly, the opportunities that lie ahead.

This chapter is ultimately about storytelling, particularly when man meets dog, so it seems right, at this point, to formally introduce a special friend of mine. She has stayed in my thoughts for many years, teaching me permanent lessons, some of which concern how to live a good life, and others are about better ways to treat my fellow man. Consistent with the best storytellers, she accomplished many of these feats often times without me knowing it. I look back now and consider how it came to be. All stories have a beginning, middle, and an end. This is the beginning of mine.

Rusty fences and deep wells

I met Kelsey when I was twenty-four years old, and in graduate school in Denton, Texas. Our first encounter was at the local Humane Society. I went there on a Friday night before they closed for the weekend, wandering through kennels filled with dogs. Some looked anxious beyond belief, as though their lives depended on being adopted (I only found out later that the shelter could not afford to keep the dogs for over a week or so before they put them down, so, their lives actually *did* depend on it). I also saw other dogs who were very aggressive. They would bark and bare their teeth when someone came close, making their presence known in full force.

Both types of dogs seemed off-base for what I was looking for, though still certainly aroused my sympathy. Most of these dogs no doubt had had a hard life so far – not enough food, water, and loving care. Perhaps they responded with the same level of intensity toward the world that the world had shown them.

A friend of mine adopted a dog only to find out later that buckshot was lodged deep into the skin of her ears. You could literally run your hand over the fleshy part and feel the buckshot. The vet said there are people out there who like to use stray dogs as target practice, and many of the kennel dogs had no doubt experienced other versions of unprovoked hostility. As many relationships go, there is a mix of awkward and sometimes aggressive relating, even among those who were devoted companions. I myself witnessed a homeless man 'teaching his dog a lesson' for trying to snatch a quick meal in the middle of a busy intersection. He ran up behind the dog and kicked him squarely between the legs. The dog, too surprised to respond at first, grabbed the sandwich and tried to eat and yelp at the same time as he ran, with his owner, away from the road.

As I think back on these scared and seemingly hardline dogs at the Humane Society, I wonder if, maybe, they were just trying to connect in the only way they knew how. It was dysfunctional by human standards, and they would most likely not be adopted. They had been taught some very poignant lessons about what the world could be like and, even more specifically, what being in the company of the human race sometimes had in store for them.

But it would be inaccurate to say that all of these would-be animal companions were marred beyond the ability to bond, and much of what I've described above can also be supposed about the would-be-owners, who had their own baggage, and also carried the hope that accompanies the prospect of a new friend. Some think that another try at connecting, this time with a cat or dog, may balance some of their experiences with the world of people. The real question is: can both person and animal companion overcome their own unique obstacles to forming a new bond?

Kelsey was in kennel 'Number 1.' She sat there, surrounded by dogs who were anxious about their survival, and others who wanted to dish out the same level of hostility they themselves had received, but she seemed remarkably cool and calm. I think I saw qualities in her that I had hoped to adopt for myself in the middle of my own 'kennel' experience of graduate school, a microcosm of the bigger living conditions. Some of my colleagues, peers, faculty, and, to be fair, myself, had varying degrees of similar anxious-aggressive behaviors that the dogs surrounding Kelsey displayed. I thought maybe if Kelsey and I pooled our resources, we might both see through our new connection.

Kelsey seemed to be the dog I was looking for: a steady companion (a Golden Retriever mix). I only noticed later that she had the greenest, human-like eyes I had ever seen. She seemed like an old soul going through this lifetime as a dog, ready for a new friend. That friend, I thought, was me. I knelt down by the gate of the cage, and told her that I would be back on Monday to take her home. I do not know if she understood what I said.

I needed to delay picking up Kelsey till Monday so I could make ready a spot for her. I went to the local hardware store to buy some fencing in order to construct a dog run. She was going to make her new home just a few feet away from the exterior door that led to my bedroom. I lived in a typical graduate student dwelling, an old, low-rent house on the edge of town. It was essentially country living. Instead of a physical address, it had a Route number and was one of two properties that sat on a hill right next to the road.

True to my word, I returned to the shelter on Monday.

Kelsey was about three months old, small, maybe twenty pounds, and very nervous as I put her in the passenger seat of my old Honda hatchback. I told her we were going home. She shook more, but eventually found my lap, where she tried to cuddle in her anxious way. We drove most of the way home like that.

This was my first real, visceral experience of her smell, her coat, and how that felt against my skin. It made me think of how a parent might first hold a newborn, wondering what the future held. And, of course, at that point, we really did not know what fate had in store for either of us.

Kelsey and I arrived home, and she did the normal dog territory marking around the area. Perhaps it was just nerves, as I would come to discover later in our friendship that Kelsey liked to travel, but the first few miles were tough for her. In later years, she sat in the back seat on long trips, and would often place her paw on the back of my seat or, if I wasn't paying attention, on my shoulder, to let me know we needed to pull over. Sometimes this would be at a McDonald's or a convenience store, but most of the times just on the side of the road. I tried to imagine Kelsey's sense of urgency based on my own internal pressures, and endeavored to accommodate her nervous bladder and bowels as we both colluded about each other's condition.

Kelsey's first night at the house did not go as planned.

I placed her out in the run I had made for her, and went to bed. The weather was not particularly hot for a May Texas evening, but I felt myself growing a little uneasy. I eventually fell asleep, only to be awakened in the middle of the night by the sound of scratching.

It had begun to rain, and Kelsey had dug her way under the fence and found the exterior door to my bedroom. I opened it, and there was my wet puppy, shaking the rain from her coat. I found a towel, dried her, and put her in the borrowed dog carrier. This didn't last long, as she began to whine. I tried to console her and go back to sleep several times, to no avail. Finally, exhausted, I lay down on the floor beside her. We both seemed to find some release and fell asleep side-by-side.

Kelsey never slept a night in the run that I made for her. Weeds grew up around it, and the fence rusted. As for ensuing sleeping arrangements, Kelsey would always crash back in my bedroom ... and I do mean 'crash.' You always knew when Kelsey was ready for a good night's sleep, because she would hit the ground with a thud. I thought, after the first night, that she would be one of those dogs who jumped into their owner's bed, and though she always had an open invitation, this was not the case (somewhat to my disappointment). In all the years we were together, she only did this once: on a cold winter's night when she leapt into my old heated waterbed. Despite the daze that often accompanies being awoken suddenly, I can still recall the tenderness of the moment. I call to mind her nuzzling hard against my body, like she was trying to draw the heat from it. She lay there for a bit, and I felt this deep sense of connection. However, the new arrangement didn't last long, as I am a restless sleeper, and maybe some combination of my snoring and rolling over helped her decide that sleeping elsewhere was a better idea. I woke the next morning, and she was in her familiar space beside the bed. This is how it would be for almost the next fourteen years.

There was something about the Hollywood version of Lassie always bunking right up against her master that stirred a certain envy in me. Isn't that what real companions do, after all? Growing up as the next to the youngest of eight kids in a small house left an indelible impression on me in terms of space, bunking, and intimacy. One of my favorite books from childhood, *Where the Wild Things Are*,[14] suggested that sleeping is always done best by lumping together with those who are dear. I didn't rediscover that notion till adulthood because, as a child, the house felt so crowded that there was little room to enjoy the rhythmic dance of being separate before connecting at the end of the day.

I had hoped I could live out a different arrangement with Kelsey. But, as I knew her better, I came to realize more that she was a dog who carried her own baggage into this relationship as well. Most likely mistreated and definitely a stray, Kelsey understood the notion of space limitations, as well as a lack of resources, in her own way, gobbling down food whenever her bowl was filled, even after coaxing more than enough table scraps from me beforehand. So, together, it seemed, we would embark on a new type of connection, one which had lessons and implications for us both. And yet, if we would ever get to a more tender place that mirrored my Lassie-like daydream of a dog who could save a boy who fell down a well, we would have to stretch in ways that our previous circumstances did not allow for.

2
Attachments – they make us real

"What is REAL?" asked the Velveteen Rabbit one day ... "Does it mean having things that buzz inside you and a stick-out handle?"
"Real isn't how you are made," said the Skin Horse. "It's a thing that happens to you. When [someone] loves you for a long, long time, not just to play with, but REALLY loves you, then you become Real." "Does it hurt?" asked the Rabbit.
"Sometimes," said the Skin Horse, for he was always truthful. "When you are Real you don't mind being hurt."
"Does it happen all at once, like being wound up," he asked, "or bit by bit?"
"It doesn't happen all at once," said the Skin Horse. "You become. It takes a long time. That's why it doesn't often happen to people who break easily, or have sharp edges, or who have to be carefully kept. Generally, by the time you are Real, most of your hair has been loved off, and your eyes drop out, and you get loose in the joints and very shabby. But these things don't matter at all, because once you are Real you can't be ugly, except to people who don't understand ... once you are Real you can't become unreal again. It lasts for always."
– Margery Williams, *The Velveteen Rabbit* or *How Toys Become Real*[1]

The Velveteen Rabbit tells the story of a toy rabbit that wants to become real. While the book was in print long before my birth, it was one of those stories that my generation grew up hearing. I recall it being told by a forward-thinking elementary school teacher, who read aloud while I sat quietly on my mat in a dimly-lit classroom, sipping chocolate milk. One of my favorite passages is the exchange between the Rabbit and his friend, the Skin Horse, above.

As a child, I remember finding the book very interesting; it even made me feel strangely warm inside when others read it aloud, like they were passing on an important secret; one that I might someday have the chance to understand. However, there was a problem when reading it on my own: I could not get past the word 'shabby' in the last paragraph; it

was as it it was underlined with a red ballpoint pen.

As a boy, shabby had a very different meaning for me. Growing up in a working-class neighborhood, shabby was the feeling you had when your family was unable to stretch an impossibly thin budget for all that was needed, or when the girl you had a crush on passed out your Free Lunch cards in homeroom. Shabby was the word that described what it was like for your parents' insecurities to become your own, only you were too young to understand how or why. Instead, you looked for something more tangible to represent – and perhaps blame – for the transformation. Shabby in this frame of reference meant feeling less than, because of having less.

While that 'less than' status could easily be pinned on having fewer material goods than those on the 'other side of the tracks,' it could also include a number of other categories to which the 'enough' measuring stick applied: education, success, and even the amount of love received. The walk away message seemed blunt, but obvious: coming up short meant being unworthy, not enough, and perhaps even unlovable.

Maybe I am a bit of a slow learner, but as I inch ever closer to fifty years old, the real meaning of the Velveteen Rabbit's exchange with the Skin Horse has finally begun to dawn on me. Perhaps shabby can have a very different, and even positive, connotation; one that Mr Webster's dictionary did not include. Maybe shabby has something to do with becoming real, because the parts deemed 'off limits' are finally brought into full view.

This may seem like a very counterintuitive approach for a generation dedicated to self-improvement; one where many of us try to recreate a better version of our original self. Most end up working very hard to create smooth and finished seams, instead of inviting others to share the obvious rough edges. The problem is some people think that the shiny, finished product is the only reason others offer us their love. It is an eye-opening experience when the genuine sharing of our tired or frayed parts is actually the reason others feel close to us, and we to them. In this context, our outer, scruffy appearance is very much more than just the mileage accrued after so many years.

Following the lead of the Velveteen Rabbit, becoming real is an occurrence that ultimately takes place because of the presence of another, in the context of important attachments made. For some, the transformation hinges on the happenings in their formative years; for others, it is in spite of them. And yet, becoming real is something most people seek. The confusing part can be how vulnerability and intimacy are intertwined, both playing significant roles. The topic is an especially important one in men's lives.

This chapter takes a closer look at attachment, the bonds formed with others, and their role in helping us become real. For men, attachment-related issues are risky; often rife with misunderstanding. The life of first a boy and then a man includes trying to honor an impossibly long list of rules, ones that are supposed to be learned and kept, or pretended to at least, by not letting others see them broken. Out of a need to both cloak perceived shortcomings and to prove that love from another is not needed, males assume a go-it-alone attitude – the supposed essence of a masculine life. The idea of relying on another as a key part of the transformation to becoming real men makes many uneasy: it seems like a violation of the rules when someone else is involved.

For some males, the presence of an animal companion bypasses much of the clutter and confusion found among attachments with our human companions. The electric fences are turned off, and many men open up in a way that does not always occur under other circumstances. The fixed rules for being a man are circumvented for the moment. In what can be a brief but important exchange, men find that the negative connotations of 'shabby' do not apply here. For some, an animal companion is a key player in helping us become real. But before getting to more of why the bond offers a unique opportunity for men, it is important to understand how attachment plays a role in the earliest connection between caregiver and child.

The strange situation

In the 1960s, researcher Mary Ainsworth devised an experiment that has come to be known as the 'strange situation,'[2] named as such because it tapped into a fundamentally distressing state of affairs: a young child being separated from a caregiver.

In Ainsworth's laboratory study, twelve-month-old children, accompanied by their mothers, were filmed as they went through a series of separations and reunions, occurring within an experimental playroom filled with toys. In what was considered the most stressful condition, mothers would unceremoniously leave the child for a few moments.

After poring over many hours of footage, Ainsworth noted various emerging patterns that reflected the quality of the interaction between mother and child; patterns which would later prove to have a lasting impact on the child's ability to form and sustain relationships. Ainsworth's work gave rise to a classification system known as 'attachment styles,' which reflected not only the first, early-life bond, but also how many people relate to others in the context of adult connections.[3] Attachment styles speak to a learned set of expectations associated with others, and also how we view ourselves. In a general sense, one can have either a secure or insecure style of attaching.

At the core of a secure attachment style are positive perceptions of ourself and others. These include messages such as: 'I am worthy of love, and when I am in need, people who love me are available and willing to offer support.' In essence, one develops trust in his or her own personal worth, and a somewhat benign view of the world of others. This type of style is derived from the experience of having a warm, responsive caregiver, who seems to intuitively read a child's needs, and responds accordingly: 'You need a little encouragement; okay, here you go.' 'You need me to back off and let you try it yourself: no problem.'

Taken together, the early encounters form a foundation that is drawn from time and again to make sense of the world and those who inhabit it. I have come to believe that the first few years of life are not the sum total of what we are, though do provide a foundation that is not easily changed. For those who grow up in circumstances leading to a more secure sense of attachment, the resultant resilience and underlying optimism are strengths upon which to draw the rest of one's life.

While a consistent

experience of having a warm, attuned caregiver helps shape the beginnings of a secure attachment style, so, too, can the absence of responsive parenting set the stage for an insecure one. Children who are more likely to develop insecure styles are prone to having caregivers unskilled in the crucial areas of reading a situation, and responding to what the child needs. This does not mean that these parents are bad people; in fact, many have the best interests of their children in mind. However, there are some roadblocks that get in the way: sometimes a lack of an attuned skill set; other times, the parents' own insecurities leak through in less than approving ways. Parents who struggle with witnessing their child's vulnerability often do so because it makes them aware of their own helplessness as a child: a situation that causes too much discomfort.

Insecure types of attachment are prone to be passed from one generation to the next. So, when a parent observes the beginnings of insecurity taking root in their child, or just the normal vulnerability that goes with being a little person in a big world, this can act as a trigger. It's difficult enough facing one's own shortcomings as a parent, whilst all the while being reminded of other crucial areas that were missed out on as a child, and it can be painful and overwhelming to see the combination in one fell swoop. The solution many decide on is the same they learned: admonishing the child to keep the potential messiness of 'weakness' firmly in check.

While there can be various types of insecure attachment scenarios, special attention needs to be paid to one in particular: the avoidant attachment style.

Avoidant type attachment

In Ainsworth's strange situation, insecurely attached children reacted to separation from their caregivers in various ways. One type showed a great deal of anxiety; some would try to follow their parent out the door; others sat pining, looking for them out the playroom window. Occasionally, children became so distressed that the experiment had to be stopped. Even the securely attached toddlers showed some signs of distress. However, there were some kids who did not seem upset at all: those who would later be classified as having an avoidant type attachment style.

Avoidant type children learn early on that showing vulnerability or needing others is off-limits, because doing so has the potential of evoking rejection or shame from someone depended on for survival – their caregiver. The rebuff could occur in subtle ways, like a parent pulling away when a child begins showing signs of a meltdown, or in very direct ways, like the child receiving verbalized messages filled with shame.

I think one of the most telling aspects of Ainsworth's work is that avoidant children had learned by the age of twelve months old to be very self-contained in moments of distress. In fact, these children were initially very confusing to the researcher, because, outwardly, they seemed cool as a cucumber when mom went away and upon her return. The kids would just keep playing in a nonchalant way, or offer a laidback version of 'What's up?' when she returned. The avoidant kids seemed the most surefooted; even more so than those children later identified as having secure attachment style. It was only subsequently discovered that, while the avoidant children's outer appearance seemed to convey a message of absolute confidence, physiological measures actually showed they were as upset as the other children.[4] They had simply learned to conceal their worries.

Current research suggests that, from the age of 12 months to about age five, children begin developing the basis for enduring attachment styles.[5] In some studies, there is a match rate of 68-75 percent between the type of attachment styles appearing in the first year of life and those found at eighteen years of age, when, as adults, the pattern continues to build upon earlier experiences. This style can influence which individuals are chosen as friends and romantic partners, and can also account for why these patterns are so hard to change: they have been around for a very long time, and can seem like the fixed reality of how connecting with someone else works. For most, these are ways of relating that cannot be easily talked out of; this is simply how people attach.

Relationship GPS

Attachment styles can be thought of as a sort of Relationship GPS, helping one navigate the sometime slippery and convoluted roads of emotional connections. Each person's Relationship GPS contains an overall global positioning, indicating how we think of ourself and significant others (ie Am I worthy of being cared for, and can others be trusted and counted on when I am in need?). The GPS also contains very specific instructions about how to handle the stress of intimacy, separations, and reunions. ('Turn left at the next pause in conversation. I am getting too personal and am feeling uncomfortable.') All these areas are where vulnerabilities may be encountered in their most raw form. The end result is a minute-by-minute orientation of the world, ourselves, and significant others.

The problem is, sometimes, error messages develop in the Relationship GPS as a result of early bonding experiences gone awry. Avoidant-styled children and adults learn to use a particular coping strategy to protect against painful moments of opening up to others. The Relationship GPS develops instructions to act über independent, never needing anyone, even when they really do. Being so self-contained keeps us safe from rejection, while still allowing for a semblance of connection with those who are loved, even if it is at a distance. At the heart of the avoidant attachment style is the notion that intimacy is dangerous, because it reveals deep personal flaws to others, which they will surely note, leading to rejection. The only way around this is to keep others at arm's length.

There are several important points to consider when looking at Ainsworth's attachment-related work. Everyone needs a responsive, warm caregiver who is attuned to our needs. When this type of relationship is absent, attachment-related difficulties can result which continue into and throughout adulthood. It is also important to consider how attachment-related issues specifically impact men; an essential topic in the understanding of the importance of man's best friend.

Men, attachment, and male socialization

Men can develop either secure or insecure styles of relating with human companions, and it may not come as a surprise to know that, if males develop an insecure type of attachment style, it will most likely be an avoidant one.[6] Avoidant-styled males attempt to minimize or constrict their emotional experience, denying a need for closeness, and being highly invested in autonomy. Opening up to others, especially in vulnerable ways, equates, in many men's minds, to being weak, breaking down, and not 'manning up' in the all too crucial moments when one's steel is put to the test. Any form of intimacy is regarded as a situation chock-full of peril.

A number of psychologists believe that males' avoidant attachment style begins at a young age, and is fully developed by middle childhood. While there are differing theories – such as family environment and parental rearing styles – to account for males' avoidant tendencies, male socialization as a contributing factor cannot be overlooked.

In his book, *Real Boys*, psychologist William Pollack discusses the ill-effects of a society out of sync with young boys.[7] Society asks them to cut ties with a caregiver's emotional support at a very young age (around two to three years old) as, at the heart of traditional male socialization, is the notion that asking for or receiving support will make a male soft. Instead, a man should embrace being solely self-sufficient, because 'real men' do not want or need others. Under these circumstances, boys are moved out of the normally age-appropriate landscape, and are instead introduced to a harsh environment marked by catchy, Nietzsche-like phrases about how what does not kill you makes you stronger. Boys and men can learn to become stronger in spite of this lack of cultural attunement, rather than because of it. The go-it-alone attitude is problematic on many fronts, including leaving boys and then men to later acquire the much-needed skillset of attuning to their own needs, and those of others.

Likewise, psychologist Ron Levant suggests that many North American men experience a condition called normative male alexithymia – the ultimate example of not being in touch with one's feelings.[8] Men appear wooden and numb; unable to track emotions or even sensations in their own bodies, struggling to register any happenings in the inner world, much less make sense of them. Not surprisingly, Levant suggests that normative male alexithymia causes significant difficulties in men's personal lives, such as marital problems, estrangement from their children, substance abuse, domestic violence, and even sexual addiction. After all, men still *have* emotions, even if they cannot identify or reconcile them when they occur. It leaves males at the mercy of intense feelings when encountering frustration, and being isolated from viable solutions that could improve their relationship outlook.

Levant argues that normative male alexithymia also results from constricting male socialization. Boys are not encouraged to develop the skills of talking about and processing emotions. In fact, parents, peers, teachers, and coaches actively discourage – and potentially unwittingly punish – boys for doing so.

This is not necessarily a male conspiracy aimed at hurting young men. All of these potential sources of support can also be duped by a skewed blueprint of how to raise boys into strong, independent men. There is the all too familiar encouragement to choke down pain and never reveal personal vulnerability to others. The outcome is that males do not develop an emotion vocabulary for when things feel intense. Levant believes this predicament is especially true for exposed feelings such as sadness, fear, and the desire for attachment with another. Without these much-needed tools, there is reduced awareness of what males feel on a regular, day-to-day basis. It is also difficult to understand another's perspective, or develop empathy, if a person cannot identify his or her own emotions.

One of the troubling outcomes of male socialization is its impact on emotions. Boys do not develop the necessary tools that will one day be called on when they begin dating, and eventually attempt to have long-term relationships. Some wake up in a cold sweat, realizing they are not sufficiently prepared to be a husband, let alone a parent one day. Many men visit with me at this point in my private practice, trying to wrestle with some of the convoluted messages they have learned about being a man. Even those able to sidestep the core trouble about being absolutely self-sufficient, and acknowledge that they want a relationship, do not know how to go about doing it. That skillset has not been developed, and there is real pressure to make up for lost time when it seems an attachment they care about hangs in the balance. When they begin venturing into what feels like the unknown world of not just sex, but emotional intimacy, more issues have to be faced.

Stephen J Bergman, MD, PhD, coined the phrase 'relational dread,' referring to the anxiety men experience when connecting with others.[9] Men fear that relating in an intimate way is against the rules. Opening up might also reveal the perceived disgraceful truth that we are not very good at this, making matters worse. Others will surely make note of our shortcomings, and will hold them against us. Male socialization tells males to be watchful, even paranoid, and to expect belittlement for anything less than stellar behavior. Often, these feelings lead to shame:

failure of any kind suggests we are less of a man.

Consider a typical exchange that occurs when a wife says to her husband, "We need to talk." In theory, this type of conversation can be the beginning of an intimate moment, a way to clear the air, and even deepen the sense of connection. However, Bergman notes that relational dread makes it anything but a close encounter for most men. Men are not supposed to have these kinds of talks; it is clearly spelled out in the handbook of traditional manhood. Not only is he in a foreign relational realm, but he is also ill-prepared, lacking the necessary implements for survival. It is the farthest thing from a safe and secure exchange, one where he can really be himself and be curious about how he feels. Instead, he has developed a default setting when pressed by his partner for a reply as to what he feels right now. He says: "Nothing: I do not feel anything."

When avoidant attachment style collides with traditional male socialization, males come to expect rejection for their perceived weakness of not living up to unrealistic standards of being solely self-sufficient and competent in all things. This adds even more reasons to the list for keeping others at a distance. By the time boys become men, they have had many years of cultural conditioning, cautioning them about letting others close. The cumulative effect of an avoidant attachment style and restrictive rules for being a man can set up a frustrating trajectory that leads to painful relationship endings, drifting apart from others, or alienation from knowing one's own true self. The skillset of getting to know our own inner world, and how to step into someone else's, is not developed. Relational skills, like empathy, perspective taking, and emotional intimacy, seem like strange concepts that are also off-limits. Untangling these matters can be very confusing, especially if it appears that males are just following what has been taught.

The majority of clients I work with in my private practice are men, and, of those, a good number have elements of avoidant attachment styles. The fact that they even make it to therapy is in and of itself noteworthy. As a general rule, males in North American have very negative attitudes about seeking support of any kind, including going to counseling.[10] I might even go so far as to say they struggle with a 'crisis of connection' – difficulty making and sustaining ties with others, as well as dialing into what they think and feel.

So, while I do not ask those visiting my practice to indicate what type of attachment style they have from the onset, it usually becomes evident shortly after they walk in my door.

It starts with a somewhat startled or apprehensive look at the point of introductions, as if I am a guide leading them into a dangerous place, and is followed by one-word answers, or stating the dire circumstances by which they felt the necessity to attend. Something important hangs in the balance: their marriage, relationships with their children, or their own general sense of malaise. A number experience somatic reactions when discussing these issues, including a fast heartbeat, an unsteady voice, or needing to excuse themselves to use the restroom.

I have also grown accustomed to edgy, defensive, or guarded reactions. Our work might start out tense, and include the client questioning my credentials, or ascertaining what right I have to poke around in their private lives. These men tell me in so many different ways that they expect to be judged, and even ostracized, for their perceived failings. After all, that is what's at the heart of an avoidant attachment style, and coming to therapy goes against the grain of everything they hold true in terms of how men in relationships operate. The idea of bringing insecurities into my office, and even talking about them with another man, can intensify the worries. This is especially true if fathers, brothers, coaches, and even friends, are part of a male chorus whose song includes criticism and judgment for anything less than absolute control.

All of this usually takes place in the first fifteen minutes of the session. Fortunately, our time can get better, and it often does. Believe me, I am sympathetic to these men's struggles. Sometimes in these tense moments, I think about a wild, injured, or cornered animal: one who does not necessarily want to appear menacing or drive others away, but who has learned to do so as a means of survival. As it turns out, man and animal are actually not after something very different – a place that feels safe. Maybe both also carry the hope that another kind of bond will come their way.

Adjusting the avoidant relational GPS

Psychologist David B Wexler suggests that, to offset the avoidant attachment challenges men face, it is important to find a safe relationship in order to work on welcoming feelings and developing relational skills.[11] Psychoanalyst Robert Karen suggests there are three ways to overcome the emotional legacy of any insecure attachment –

• Having a loving, supportive figure as a child to counterbalance other painful experiences
• Being in long-term therapy as an adult
• Having a stable, understanding spouse[12]

I would add a fourth to the list –

• The presence of a trusted animal companion

My career has been devoted to studying the intersection of attachment-related issues and problematic male socialization. In my clinical work, I customarily ask clients about the experiences in the formative years that have shaped how they function, and see themselves now as adult men. Topics usually include how bonds were made and sustained in the families they grew up in, and what troubles were encountered, including overly strict notions of what a man was supposed to be.

I have also learned from experience to ask about the pivotal place of others who acted as counterbalances to the challenges present. The rule of thumb is that everyone needs at least one good presence in their life to endure the difficulties of growing up. What I have seen over the years is that the crucial presence may take on many forms, including an occasionally-seen relative, a friend, coach, teacher, and, of course, an animal companion.

A client once shared some of the harsh realities of being a boy in his dysfunctional family. On one hand was the long list of his father's interpersonal struggles, which made him too scary and unreliable to approach. On the other hand, his emotionally-distant mother was unable to respond in a way that was needed. Then there was my client, a child caught in the middle, and alone in overwhelming circumstances. He found relief by slipping away from the chaos inside the house and spending time with his dog. In those moments, he felt free. My client recalled with a clarity that had been sustained over the years the tangible sensation of petting his dog and hugging him in the way that he hoped someone could offer him. It was the bond with his animal companion that helped him make it through tough times.

Developmental psychologists have argued for more than thirty years that childhood experiences with animal companions can help teach valuable relationship lessons.[13] For instance, a childhood dog has been compared to having a confidant, sibling, and teacher. A child may feel safer sharing a range of emotions, such as being angry, scared, and upset, that, in most other contexts, seems off-limits.

Some argue that the bond also imparts to the child lessons about empathy, and that being with an animal companion facilitates the process of reading non-verbal cues even better than when interacting with a human companion. The difference is that most dogs have a safe, but also very honest and direct way of relating; they let us know about being out of bounds. These findings suggest that the bond can help a person become more skilled at making and sustaining connections.

The power of the bond keeps the relational part of some men alive, even if they have experienced harsh male socialization. In other circumstances, it helps that relational part flourish.

One recent study looked at the effect of dog ownership in elderly Japanese men.[14] Those men – who owned their first dog at an early age, and other dogs later – were more likely to report a closer degree of connection and depth in their interpersonal relationships with their human neighbors and friends. It was also found that the same men became more likely to accept social support from their partners. The human-canine bond taught these men that it is not only okay, but also rewarding, to let others in, and that meaningful connections could be a part of life from childhood to old age.

Writing about the bond

One of the reasons I am sympathetic to my male clients is that I can identify with some of their struggles. Case in point, I didn't realize how hard it would be to write this book, and it went through so many drafts over a number of years, each one being not quite right. It finally dawned on me that I was only sharing parts of my story in the safe way I had come to rely upon: in the form of a dry textbook explanation. To the reader of these early drafts, it seemed I was held up in the gray matter portion of my brain. "Where was the emotional connection?" some would ask after re-reading it, now for the fifth time.

I felt so surprised when receiving this feedback, because I knew the level of emotional intensity when writing the book, and then later reading parts to my wife. My voice would crack as I read aloud. Even if my feelings seemed hidden behind word choice or the style used on the printed page, I thought each still offered hints of what really lies below, which is part of the problem in being an avoidant styled male. Amid the emotional disguises learned over the years, there is still the hope that someone will see through them, understanding in a way that feels safe to share. Even shedding a tear, the ultimate display of male vulnerability, is still a form of condensing emotions into a small ambiguous package, one that seemed confusing to others and prone to misinterpretation. While the full scope of what I felt may have remained uncertain to others, for me, I am clear about the deep ties I have toward my animal companions, a fact that I am open about, and yet still reluctant to share all the details of.

I am a private person by nature, but being a man who has also experienced much of the traditional male socialization I have studied for years adds to my somewhat reserved style. It is something I have struggled with for a long time. Ex-girlfriends from my twenties and thirties had, on more than a few occasions, seemed a bit surprised when they witnessed a more vulnerable part of me they had never encountered while we dated. It wasn't that my inner emotional life was entirely lacking, it was just that all of what I felt was not always apparent, and sometimes far from it. "I didn't realize you really cared that much about me or our relationship," marks the exchange in more than one of those post-break-up discussions. I was not always consciously trying to conceal what was there, or maybe it had just become an engrained way of being. However, I knew that there was a tendency to abbreviate my emotional world into subtle gestures and nuances that I still hoped would be recognized, which did not help things either.

I suppose it should come as no surprise that, when purposefully trying to tell about personal important connections, even with my animal companions, there is a barrier, a veil that only allows a glimpse of what lies behind it. It is all too easy for me to revert to another form of emotional condensation: as a narrator who relies too heavily on others' stories to convey my own. Offering a clear and unfettered view seems like a risk. After all, men are not supposed to overshare their tender feelings. To do so comes with the danger of being branded soppy or not man-enough.

I finally decided that I needed to move out of my comfort zone if I was going to complete this book. It meant ignoring those rules about 'being a man' that have been drilled into my head since I was a boy; maybe the willingness to do so is in and of itself some type of testimonial about the bond. What I try to do is strike a balance between offering explanations for why the bonds with animal companions are so important to men, while also not leaning too far in a cerebral direction in a way that obscures the heart of what I am trying to convey.

The latter is the core element of the bond's magic, intertwined with the realness found in the everyday events unfolding around us. Living, loving, and yes, saying good-bye to friends and family who die make us who we are. They invite us to move out from behind the well-worn personas, in order to experience the bond in an unfettered way, and perhaps also to share its power with others.

Dog have three sets of eyelids

I always tried to be polite, professional, and even warm with those I worked with, but I knew, down deep, I also kept a safe distance. In this case, I had shared the same office in a group private practice for more than four years, but the staff confided to my wife, who also worked there, "We don't know him at all." To counter this perception, she fed them bits and pieces of my humanity without me knowing: "He likes zombie movies, does celebrity impressions (badly), and most of all loves dogs." The

last part would come in handy from time to time.

Over the course of my work as a psychologist, I have learned to almost never comment on a client's physical appearance, even when they want me to; it seems like a no-win situation, especially when it involves some type of self-deprecating comment: "See how fat I have gotten?" But when the young man I had worked with for a few years walked into my office, looking very skinny, I said, "You look thinner than I can ever remember." Expecting the impromptu conversation starter to launch into a discussion, he instead stated that his dog had unexpectedly died over the weekend.

This intelligent man was very much on his own. In fact, I had seldom ever met anyone who was so painfully alone. His solace was found in the company of his animal companion. The only emotions he ever displayed directly in sessions were frustration that others did not understand his complicated inner world. There were times when I also felt like I was just getting to know the real him, and it was always hard doing so: having to coax him into speaking for thirty minutes before maybe we would have a dialogue for the last fifteen of the meeting.

But, today, he sat across from me and volunteered that unexpected medical complications had taken 'His best friend,' the only one who really understood him. I had never seen him cry. But one tear after another rolled down his cheeks for nearly the entire time we met. He spoke of the emptiness he felt, the guilt for not spending more time together the past few weeks, because he was utilizing the connection with his animal companion to finally reach out to others. He never inquired about my personal life, but today he asked if I had a dog. Upon replying 'Yes,' he said, "Hug her for me." I remember going home and giving Sadie an embrace that had a surprising level of intensity.

I felt affected by that session the rest of the day.

I was surfing the internet about random topics relating to dogs, and read an article about canine friends having three sets of eyelids. Vets suggest it's a muscle that dogs voluntarily open or close to protect their eyeballs; like a windshield-washer that sweeps away debris. I think it is also used so they can see us clearly when it seems no one else can.

That night I had a dream. I watched as mystical figure dressed in black, who sat atop a horse, take to the air. The rider floated on the clouds, and began calling home all of the dogs and cats, gathering them in one fell swoop into a long procession stretching across the sky. Some were the forgotten ones who had been victims of neglect or abuse; others had just passed away. Listening closely I could hear each individual cat meow or dog bark in a joyful way; when hearing them as a group they made a song so sweet and powerful that it bordered on being an angelic hymn, one that grew louder and beyond the capacity for my human ears to receive.

The ultimate strange situation

Animal companions are a healthy and helpful presence in mens' lives, though the bond does not always begin in the formative years. Some discover the power of the bond in young adulthood, as a dog becomes a trusted sidekick, while others find it an indispensable go-to connection when they marry or have kids. The stories that peak my curiosity now, which may be directly due to my own age, involve reports by middle-aged men about how their dogs became an anchor in their sometimes tumultuous lives. These challenges may include a painful divorce, estrangement from grown children, a lifetime of operating under masculine misconceptions, or a social support network dwindling to the size of a postage stamp. Equally as important are those men who report a good life, finding success in work and love, and yet still have a special place in their hearts for their canine companions. With the accumulation of stories about man's best friend, I have since made it a standard part of my clinical practice to listen for this sometimes overlooked connection. Some men are waiting to be told it is okay to talk about the bond. When sensing it is safe, some do.

Considering the various points about attachment and male socialization mentioned above, it seemed like a natural next step in my work to reflect on 'when man meets dog,' and turned my full attention to research regarding animal companions, especially in men's lives. With the help of colleagues and friends, one outcome was the book, *Men and Their Dogs: A New Understanding of Man's Best Friend*,[15] the first academic book focusing on how dogs play a pivotal role in male health and well-being, across the lifespan from boyhood to old age. At various places, I share findings from that book, and other related research from experts in the field of human-animal interaction.

In order to give this book a specific touchstone throughout, I also discuss the results from a nationwide survey of one hundred adult males. I asked men to share their experience of attachment, loss, and sustaining a continuing bond with their dogs. For example, in terms of attachment, compare their closest human and animal companions, indicating how securely they felt with each type of attachment. In 62 percent of cases, an attachment with an animal companion was labeled as "almost always' a secure one. By comparison, only 10 percent of men labeled their closest human companion in the same way. Instead, the most common classification for a human bond was "sometimes." That is, men perceived that the attachment, even with their closest human companion, was sometimes secure and sometimes not.

The results suggest that there can be different styles of attaching between the two types of companions. While some may be more disposed to act from an avoidant approach, in most circumstances with friends, family, and co-workers, there are those special bonds which allow men to move beyond both the usual perceptions and guarded expectations. When in the presence of an animal companion who allows for a feeling of safety and security, the typical insecurities and accompanying responses are deactivated. What emerges is a different type of encounter. These respites keep alive the hope that real human connections can be made; they also provide a powerful bond that can literally help us transform into real people.

In the broadest sense, an animal companion offers a relationship that may be considered, in most other cases, the ultimate 'strange situation' for men. A relationship is what many men are taught to simultaneously wish for and fear, and these are the competing sets of feelings underlying the confusing layers of being a man. However, making and sustaining a connecting relationship with our animal companions does not feel so strange or confusing. Instead, it seems safe and simple. Experiencing this type of bond offers a step in the direction of becoming real men, and more than the cutout versions of masculine caricatures that others often see.

Pure love

There are a number of reasons why interaction with animal companions is safe. One is based on what psychoanalyst Sigmund Freud referred to as the remarkable 'pure love' qualities that characterize our relationships with animal companions.[16] 'Pure love' connections are defined by the sense of unconditional love or acceptance received from an animal companion. Animal companions witness our vulnerabilities, having full access to areas that may have been dormant for a long time, and those that have never made an appearance before now. The happy tail wagging, gentle nuzzle, and joy of play are all responses to the real, caring moments that are shared.

Many people walk away with the sense that all facets of our being are worth having a relationship with, not just the ones dressed up and put on display. It is a life-changing experience, being able to open up without having to prepare for what normally follows in a man's world of relationships: the worry of being misperceived and thought less of, because of breaking the rules of manhood. Even those with more avoidant type attachment styles, who have spent a lifetime slowly warming to others, may quickly register the potential for this new type of bond. Some will take it in bit by bit, over time. Others allow the process to go faster. Both approaches ultimately lead to the same result, the experience of something so substantial that it can only be described in terms of pure love. For many, this will be the first time of receiving such a gift.

Freud also remarked, "Dogs love their friends and bite their enemies, quite unlike people, who are incapable of pure love, and always have to mix love and hate in their object relations."[17] Dogs lack the ambivalence that all humans struggle with on a daily basis. Once you are a made-man in a dog's mind, you are one for life. Their love does not waver. You will not receive memos saying,

"Your services are no longer needed," or text messages saying, "I love you, but I am no longer *in* love with you." Sometimes with human friends, family, and significant others, there can be a much wider range of feelings and accompanying behaviors, which can vary greatly from love to hate; safety to fear. Referring to the human-animal bond questionnaire mentioned a moment ago, the men surveyed only considered the connection even with their perceived closest human companion as safe "sometimes." That can leave a wide margin for anxiety and doubt. Males, especially the ones with avoidant attachment styles, not only register these discrepancies, but also have the tendency to over-exaggerate them. Predictability is one of those quintessential psychological qualities everyone needs, especially if our early attachment experiences teach us to worry about abandonment or rejection that feels beyond our control. If loved ones are too inconsistent, it activates very old relationship GPS files warning to be on the lookout for real or imagined trouble ahead.

Canine companions, by comparison, are more consistent in the ways they relate. In the human and animal companion attachment survey, the majority of men considered the bond with dogs to be safe and secure "almost always." 'Almost always' describes not only our perceived level of security, but also the consistency with which animal companions respond. While they are not automatons designed to repeat the same actions day in and day out, the range of reactions they display are both less extreme and less random. You almost always know what you're going to get from canine friends, who become an emotional constant on which it seems safe to rely. While some human connections can sometimes be complicated by inconsistency and contaminated by frustration, disappointment, and worry, the bond with canine companions is instead distilled to a purer level of love. Pure love relationships are without ambivalence and inconsistency. The care received feels clear and steady. For someone with insecure attachment issues, the power of having a constant presence in your life cannot be underestimated.

However, pure love relationships are not only about what is received, but also, sometimes even more importantly, about what is offered: an acceptance and a willingness to stay sturdy in the face of someone else's difficulties and periods of stressful transitions. It can be especially challenging for avoidant styled men to offer pure love, because it causes confusion on multiple levels. The Relationship GPS Rulebook clearly states that rejection is the expected outcome for our own shortcomings, and implies that is also how one should react to others showing their own rough edges, and having momentary meltdowns.

It may seem that such worries are an irrelevant topic with animal companions, and there might be the perception that all dogs are born a paragon of stability; unfortunately, that generalization does not account for those who suffer from an array of troubles, like separation anxiety or aggressive tendencies. There are a number of canine behavioral specialists offering advice on dogs who seem to love too much, or at least not in ways that are healthy. For dogs who have experienced prior neglect, abandonment, or even abuse, a special type of care is needed in order to get back on track. Even under normal human-animal bond conditions, there will be times when the counted-on consistency of a canine companion gives way to something different. It can involve breaking-in periods of being a puppy or the struggles of an elderly dog whose functionality has declined. In these circumstances, it is our turn to offer an extra portion of care. Part of our ability to do that comes from pure love, or at least our attempts at providing it. Even if Freud was correct in saying that human beings are incapable of sustaining pure love on a consistent basis, there is something very important about still trying. Not only does it help our friend, it also changes us in a fundamental way.

When Kelsey and then Sadie came into my life, a different set of challenges accompanied each. As a puppy, Kelsey and I bonded quickly, but she still had her moments, sometimes being leery of me. I came to realize that this had to with situations of uncertainty, like transitions involving new places, people, and not knowing what to expect. When she was anxious, there were two modes of operation – roll over and show her belly in the submissive position, or bare her teeth when folks got a little too close. I wondered about – and also empathized with – how her past experiences shaped the need to be so cautious. During one of these anxious rounds, I tried to diffuse the tension with a playful gesture, gently taking hold of her tail. It was meant to convey, "I come in peace and mean no harm; it's play time." But the message she received was very different. Kelsey turned in an instinctive way, as if she was preparing to fend off an enemy on the Serengeti Plain. I quickly discovered that the ability to lightly and playfully touch her tail without her preparing for battle was the most accurate barometer of when she felt safe in uncertain conditions.

Kelsey and I moved several times over our fourteen years together. This included graduate school, and new jobs that took us on a tour around and in and out of state. During all of these transient times, the tail touching was the best gauge of her being 'okay.' It was often the case that, when we first moved to a new place, or there were new people involved, she would regress for a short period, and it was once again off-limits. If I did not pick up on her anxiety, she let me know straight away. I respected that. There was a cleanness about this way of communicating. I always knew right where things stood – could I touch the tail or not? There was not much ambiguity in our relationship. Deep down I knew our bond was still solid, no matter what the situation, but sometimes she needed a little extra care that included more understanding on my part.

While in moments of uncertainty, Kelsey had a more outwardly aggressive response. Sadie, on the other hand, expressed her initial anxiety as a puppy through an attempt to chew up almost everything I owned: shoes, couches, remote controls, and spectacles, to name but a few. In fact, Sadie's Border Collie teethmarks still decorate the dining room chairs I painstakingly handmade out of quarter sawn oak, using traditional mortise tendon joinery. I used to think these chairs would outlive me by two lifetimes, but maybe not if Sadie had something to say about it. I remember coming home from work and discovering what had happened; I nearly burst a vein in my forehead. At the time, the thought of redoing my handiwork seemed far more than I had bargained for. And even if I fixed things, it did not guarantee that the flashing neon sign that only Sadie could read, directing her to 'chew here' would disappear. Later, when Sadie felt more secure at home, and it no longer seemed as though we were trapped in an afterschool special for troubled teens, I put away any thought of removing those teething marks, and they now stand as a testament to our earned connection.

Real relationships mean real work, usually on both sides of the relationship equation. That is why they are so special. Becoming real is an occurrence that ultimately takes place because of the presence of another, and in the context of the important attachments that are made. Each party learns to give and receive. While experiencing initial moments of pure love, there is also the realization that it is something which takes its own unique shape over time, in a bond that is tried and true. There is work involved in order to settle into a consistent rhythm of care, and even with that established, there will be the occasional bumps. Our attempts to achieve an approximation of pure love are reflected across all of these situations. These dynamics have their own special meaning in the lives of men who struggle with avoidant attachment issues, and have been influenced by constricting male socialization.

It is hard to capture, much less condense, the essence of two heartfelt bonds that have stretched over nearly half of my life. If Kelsey or Sadie could speak English, maybe they could offer the right words to describe what the finished product of pure love looks like from their point of view. What I do know is that my sometimes-stumbling efforts to both give and receive has helped me find the better part of myself, something not usually seen or experienced by those around me. I am able to care deeper and more openly than before. When there were missteps by either party, I bounced back quicker. My attempts at pure love for Kelsey and Sadie have led me to a place that I did not know existed previously. Perhaps the best testament I can offer to pure love is found in the pages that follow, woven through a lifetime of shared encounters, ones that ultimately allowed me to become more real.

"What is REAL?" asked the Velveteen Rabbit ...
"Does it hurt?"
"Does it happen all at once?"
"It doesn't happen all at once," said the Skin Horse. "You become. It takes a long time ... once you are Real you can't become unreal again. It lasts for always."

What is real? Does it hurt? Does it take a long time? These are all questions worth pondering in the context of any important bond, especially those characterized by pure love. When reflecting on all that occurs over the course of a connection from its beginnings, to settling into a rhythm of relating, and finally finding a way to face its eventual loss, there are many openings for pure love to enter and take hold. When it does, pure love permanently changes us: "Once you are real you can't become unreal again. It lasts for always." Maybe both Kelsey and Sadie became more real because we stuck together through thick and thin. They came into their own as we struggled and took care of each other.

They also gave me a gift that I can in no way repay. The chance to love and be loved by two special someones for a long, long time, and by doing so, bit by bit, that has changed me for the better.

3

The American Adam

"Guys like us, that work on ranches, are the loneliest guys in the world.
They got no family. They don't belong no place. They come to a ranch
an' work up a stake, and the first thing you know they're poundin' their
tail on some other ranch. They ain't got nothing to look ahead to …
A guy needs somebody – to be near him. A guy goes nuts if he ain't
got nobody. Don't make no difference who the guy is, long's he's with
you. I tell ya, I tell ya a guy gets too lonely an' he gets sick."
– John Steinbeck, *Of Mice and Men*

When I look at the scrapbook of photos from my childhood, a few things stand out. The first is that I never really seemed comfortable in front of the camera. My signature style of posing usually involved squinting, as if the sun was perpetually in my eyes. The second is that my parents would often dress my brother and me as cowboys, and, as cowboys, an imaginary Wild West appeared in our backyard. I remember the pretend shootouts, and using fallen tree limbs to make horses. We also watched a lot of Western-themed television shows. All of these experiences increased my desire to sit under the big sky and discover the real West with my father, on a trip he promised we would one day take.

My father and I never compared notes on 'being a cowboy,' but I have a feeling we shared some of the same ideas. Though he was not from one of your more traditional cowboy states, and neither did he don over-stylized western attire, I sometimes thought of him as a cowboy when he pulled away in one of the convertible sports cars he had spent hours trying to rebuild or maintain. When he was behind the wheel, he seemed almost free. Maybe the responsibilities of trying to support sometimes up to eight children at a time, or what seemed like the never-ending conflict between him and my mother, could be temporarily put aside. The easy, but seldom seen peace while driving was also helped by the possibility that the most recently cobbled together clunker had a real chance of making it back home. And if I was the lucky passenger, with the top down, the sky *did* seem bigger; almost like we were taking that trip he was never able to deliver. Cowboys hold a special place in my mind.

As I grew up, I also developed a love for driving. One of my favorite cars was also one of the worst: a 1971, two-seat roadster that had sleek lines, but was already well past its prime when I owned it. Over our time together, it developed an even more temperamental personality. On cold days, sleet and snow came in through the gaps where the window glass did not quite meet the convertible top. This make of car also had a notorious reputation for electrical issues and short-circuiting. Besides the horn sounding at random times (behind someone at a traffic light, say), on rainy days, the windshield wipers would often stop working. It was not an uncommon occurrence to have to use my arm as a makeshift substitute as I drove.

I don't know how many times I ended up stranded due to mechanical failure, but, for all its trouble, when the driving conditions were right, I felt like I was living my own version of riding the range. It was just the road and me in a four-wheeled form of escapism. Driving promoted a sense of being entirely self-sufficient, and it felt like I was fulfilling one of the prime directives of what it meant to be a man – riding off into the sunset, alone ... until, that is, the car broke down, and I had to find a way to the nearest gas station to call someone for a ride.

For all the illusionary sense of manliness generated by being behind the wheel, it was not until later, when my animal companions found their place in the passenger seat, that driving took on a whole new meaning. After all, every man needs a sidekick and someone to share the trail with. The bond with an animal companion sidesteps many of the challenges other forms of friendship often present, and, oddly enough, does not break the rules of being totally self-sufficient, either. Having this type of connection is not the same as needing one, even if you really do. The time spent with man's best friend is not regarded as burdensome; not weighed down by the man-enough rulers forever sizing you up in all areas of your life. I know this may sound over the top, and it is. Nonetheless, it is hard to explain what a relief it is to be free of the confusing and frustrating extra layers, even for a few moments.

The bond is also far more than simply a collusion with masculine hang-ups concerning intimacy. Men regard animal companions as providers of a unique sense of accompaniment, which lifts us from the daily grind. We cannot achieve the same experience by slipping off into a self-sufficient fantasy, or disappearing deep within a man-cave alone. Instead, we share a walk, we play catch, and we ride down the road together. For these reasons alone, a canine companion occupies a very special place in a man's life. Even now, I find genuine peace in the company of my animal friends. Our bond is a deep connection that is at the same time a respite from all the internal dialogue.

In this chapter I would like to talk about how contemporary culture sets the stage for the unique exchange between man and dog. The story I want to tell is about the American Adam, a mythological figure that blends rules for masculinity with the American Dream. Discussing the various sons of Adam, one of who includes the cowboy, also sets the stage for understanding the importance of man's best friend.

The American Adam

Like any country invested in its own mythos, America has created its own unique cultural identity, many of the stories about which concern a form of exceptionalism. It was the underdog colony that won its independence; built a nation that spanned a continent from sea to shining sea, and even landed a man on the moon. For each of these events, hard-working individuals pooled their talents so that something unique could emerge. Given the precedent, it only seems right that other forms of exceptionalism be emphasized as well. The one focused on in this chapter pertains to the unrealistic rules that guide men on how they are supposed to *be* men; something I will refer to as 'masculine exceptionalism.'

I also borrow a phrase from literary critic R W B Lewis, who, in 1955, coined the expression the 'American Adam.'[1] The American Adam is a mythical persona that can be traced back to the birth of the nation; the very roots of the American Dream are based upon vast opportunity and self-sufficiency. This Adam embodies an exceptional and heroic quality. He acquires these characteristics from his birthplace, another type of Eden that is untainted by the various influences associated with the old world. Because his roots are in the New World, he is free from the constraints of the past which mark other men in Europe, such as class affiliation, prior traditions, and any system that attempts to impose absolutes. Instead, Adam is free – a romantic explorer who lives in the moment. He sits alone in a unique place among other men, fulfilling a manifest destiny that lies over each new horizon.

Lewis traces the various faces of Adam in the forms of heroic literary characters appearing throughout the 18th, 19th, and 20th centuries. Drawing on the likes of James Fenimore Copper, Emerson, Thoreau, Hawthorne, Melville, and Henry James, Adam's genealogy includes the frontiersmen, a sailor, a cowboy, and a rugged individualist. Each protagonist also represents how men responded to the challenges of the times in exceptional ways, a blueprint for how an American man ideally displayed masculinity. While the stories and characters change over the decades, at heart, they are the same. Masculine exceptionalism is framed as becoming 'your own man,' an expression of the American Dream at work in masculine lives. The American Adam embraces individualism and self-determination as integral parts of his identity. He makes his own choices, not cowing down or conforming to anyone else. Adam thinks, acts, and lives on his own terms. The unique blend of manhood is woven from the very fabric of the American mythos depicted in novels, and later on the big screen. This becomes the target every man shoots for. The American Adam is the embodiment of masculine exceptionalism.

It is important from the onset to recognize that American Adam's guiding principles are aspirational in nature, or even a lofty ideal. No one really achieves them, and it is more the case that the best part of a man rises up for a few proud moments. It is easy for the icon to be confused with an achievable, sustained reality, and, if taken too far, his virtue can become his vice. I remember so many of the movies, shows, and books from growing up that pitted the uncompromising hero against the town villain. In each of these scenarios, the various likenesses of the American Adam always won in the end, because he did not waver from his personal code.

This made such an impression on me as a young man trying to find my way. On one hand, it left me inspired, but on the other, it set a tone for developing a sometimes rigid or moralistic perspective that any concession is the same as a deep personal compromise, constituting an unacceptable and unmanly failure. Being a man was seen in very dichotomous terms: the right way and then the wrong way. I thought the solution was to fight every perceived injustice in the same way. I also believed that masculinity was a state of being that, once achieved, never wavered across any situation. The hero on

the big screen is the same across all circumstances, so I thought that meant I could eventually be so, too.

In reality, the state of one's sense of masculinity is not like crossing the finish line, a complete set-in-stone product never to be adjusted or re-examined.[2] It is a normal occurrence for men to rethink some notions of being a man over the course of their life, and includes having more situation-specific considerations, realizing that the rules are not as hard and fast as one might have imagined at a younger age. Otherwise it can be difficult to not regard everyday decisions concerning work and love in dire terms – is one living up to the legacy of real men who went before, or not? Am I a man, or not? Case in point, even if a man is the boss at work, this does not equate to following the same script at home with his wife and children. Some men will question whether they are compromising their manhood by simply adjusting the volume on how they do things. There are a number of other examples in which stretching the same model of masculinity across every dilemma is problematic.

The other day, I was at a museum with my infant son. Another child ran by and manhandled one of the displays. The museum attendant, assuming by the boy's proximity that I was his father, approached, frantically waving his arms and speaking in an aggressive tone, "Sir, do not let your child touch the exhibit!" The old rules I knew as a young man stated very clearly that the only correct response to a hostile one, even if it was misplaced, was to offer a reply with the same level of antagonism, otherwise, someone would be one-upping my sense of being a man. While I am still fully capable of stumbling over my own rigidity in these moments, I tried calmly explaining that he was not my child and moved on. What was not so neat and tidy was the old feeling of needing to set things right. In hindsight, as I try to remind myself, instead of a one-size-fits-all approach, there is a range of responses that can be applied without also constituting as a sellout. In fact, there is strength in being able to stay within the bounds of one's beliefs, *and* maintain flexibility.

Man troubles

Masculinity is even more complex these days because the ideal version of manhood is further exaggerated. While I can see my middle-aged peers struggling, it is very different for younger generations. It was not enough, apparently, to compare oneself to literary icons from the past, reinvented for each subsequent generation over much of the 20th century. Now, each everyday hero must have twenty-five-inch biceps and a six-pack, and if that status cannot be achieved naturally, there are always performance-enhancing products to help create a tangible expression of manhood. During the late 20th and early 21st centuries, the American Adam also got a whole lot tougher: where previously one bullet used to stop a man, today, it is shrugged off like a pesky mosquito. The contemporary version of masculine exceptionalism involves increased physical prowess, as well as other aspects of extreme success.

This new type of superman has its roots in the 20th century's growing cultural value placed on celebrity, vast fortune, and personal well-being. It is hard to imagine the preceding time in America, when one did not demand the allotted fifteen minutes of fame, which, at one time, seemed undignified. Needless to say, times have changed, and the expectation is to achieve great things at an early age. Maybe this will involve cashing in on a dotcom, or selling your start-up business for a huge profit right out of college. There is an attitude that not only should every man be able to achieve fame and fortune, but also that this should be accomplished easily. This is a vast departure from the original Adam's self-made male identity, in which any significant achievement is a result of blood, sweat, and tears over long periods of time. Real effort is at the heart of the American Dream, where working hard enough could eventually change your position in life. Today's men are not only more inclined to mistake a video game character with who they should be, but we try to sort through the challenges of success and masculinity entirely on our own.

While a self-reliant quality has always characterized Adam's sense of masculinity, now, it goes much further, and there is a new comfort in being absolutely on one's own. Isolation becomes synonymous with being man. In fact, this state is actually preferred, and seen as a mark of true individuality. The new essence of male success is equated with doing it all on our own. Sociologist Michael Kimmel notes that, whereas brotherhood and fraternity once occupied a central role in the history of the American male experience, competition for perceived limited resources during the 19th and 20th centuries – coupled with a growing sense of homophobia – make emotional connection between men suspect.[3] When it does occur, it takes the form of angrily tag-teaming women, as they have become the focal point of men's frustration and misplaced blame for their own limited success. Kimmel points out that the new guiding credo has become: "Bros before hoes."[4] In the 20th century and beyond, these various issues of success, isolation, and conflicted masculinity have been causing real problems for men.

Psychologists and researchers first recognized the quandary men face in the later part of the 20th century. One tangible response is the establishment of Division 51 of the American Psychological Association, the Society for the Psychological Study of Men & Masculinity, in the mid-1990s. Division 51 takes the stand that gender roles – the societal rules for how men and women should conduct themselves – are largely based on problematic stereotypes that ultimately prove contradictory and impossible to achieve. This is not to say that the American Adam has lost a step or two over the centuries but, rather, that no one can really hope to realize or sustain the new standard of being an ideal man. Instead of

a hero, the sons of Adam secretly begin to feel like misfits.

Male socialization leaves men confused and in a double bind. The temptation is to mistake self-reliance for total self-sufficiency, and feel pressure to keep any form of vulnerability firmly in check. While potentially benefiting from various types of social support, men simultaneously feel blocked from accessing them. Needless to say, these acquired practices often have a negative impact on relationships with significant others, friends, and family. Making matters worse, without a male buddy or social network to work through some of these concerns, many males further distort these issues in their own heads. It is tough enough trying to fill the shoes of a cultural idol, but at least there was someone to lament its impossibility with before!

More than two-and-a-half centuries separate today's man from the original American Adam, but the later incarnation with a chip on his shoulder is still at work today. Institutions and resource groups, such as media, schools, sports, peers, and even unwitting parents, assume supporting roles advocating for unobtainable masculine exceptionalism. The resulting influence has an emphasis on keeping outliers – those who do not measure up – in check. The irony is that most everyone is an outsider when measured by such stringent requirements.

These issues teach males from a very early age to keep perceived shortcomings in check and out of view. While today's Adam uses catchy phrases, and has bumper stickers reflecting a confident, go-it-alone attitude, 'Fake it till you make it' may be a more appropriate slogan for snowboards and muscle cars.

The American Adam in the 20th-21st centuries faces a new 'normal'; something different than ever before. There is an impossible standard by which men size up their success, especially when it becomes entangled with issues of masculinity. The ultimate conclusion is to feel unworthy; a ne'er-do-well. Today's men surpass the original American Adam in only one area: by being exceptionally alone.

Men's group

My wife has what seems like an impossibly long list of friends. I still cannot remember all of their names. She gets frustrated with my inability to draw from the flow chart that I store in my head in order to keep her friends and their back-stories straight. "Who is that again?" I ask, "… is that the one who lives in Phoenix or Portland?" "No, no, no …" she says, "Why can't you ever remember any of my friends …?"

Her social escapades even sometimes include attending a women's group, for her own personal growth and edification. By comparison, my social network is lackluster. A single posit could easily contain an elaborate, color-coded diagram of my social web of connections with plenty of room left over for additional footnotes and accompanying bylines. That is, if you don't count men's group.

My participation in this group started one evening after watching a TV show about a

middle-aged man who seemed to be experiencing life challenges similar to my own. Besides feeling the strange compulsion of wanting to offer the man in the story a hug, I turned to my wife and said, "He and I should be in a men's group." After that, each time a new fictional character passes my way meeting the group's admittance criteria, he is automatically granted honorary membership.

A charter member was the BBC version of Kurt Wallander, a Swiss police detective played by Kenneth Branagh, who tries to make peace with his estranged father while being consumed by his work. Then there is the deeply conflicted Don Draper/Dick Whitman during the first few seasons of *Mad Men*. Will Don ever let anyone really see who he is? One of my favorites is Walter White, a middle-aged teacher inclined to break bad in an attempt to feel alive.

You might wonder why I would resort to such a fantasy-based circle of friends. That is easy to answer. It takes so much to establish a friendship with another male, and it is much easier, instead, to just imagine how, in the context of a movie or show, a member of a men's group tells their story uninterrupted, while I vicariously share their pain.

I remember growing up watching the movie *Cool Hand Luke*. The story has many themes, including men's friendship amid difficult prison conditions. Luke is played by Paul Newman who, on his arrival, immediately courts the competitive rivalry of a much bigger and fiercer character played by George Kennedy. Tensions continue to rise between Newman and Kennedy, until they eventually square off in a makeshift boxing ring. While Newman is outweighed by more than fifty pounds, and is no match for his opponent, each time he is knocked down, he doggedly gets back up. This goes on for an excruciatingly long stint, and Newman is bloody, bruised, and nearly unconscious on his wobbly legs. Amid this tenacious exchange, Kennedy's character begins to gain a new respect for the man he is pummeling. He even starts to feel somewhat sympathetic and tender toward his newly-minted friend as he helps carry Newman out of the ring.

The story sticks with me, because this is one of the versions of what it takes to add a new male friend to the roster: an extended period of posturing and pummeling, all of which may or may not lead to the possibility of earned mutual respect. I have been down that road. Given that most men are not taught the skillset needed to sidestep any of the seemingly required prerequisites of friendship, at some point in my life I began hearing the echoes of a different movie character. This time, the world-weary middle-aged one played by Danny Glover in the *Lethal Weapon* movies: "I am getting too old for this shit."

Another path to male friendship I have experienced can best be described as an emotionally lop-sided one. I have acquired a few relationship skills honestly through personal work and reflection, as well as some through my training as a psychologist. I am not sure why the latter feels like cheating, because obtaining that set was no easy task, but it still seems a bit similar to taking relationship steroids. In either case, I have learned that men slowly warm to the possibility of having male friends who actually listen to them. The part that gets frustrating for me is waiting for my turn to be heard. It is too often the case that once my potential newbie friend starts talking, he does not register the magical word reciprocate, or the attempts to do so are poor. At that point, I quickly revaluate my expectations as I listen to my own soliloquy.

I remember once during a long weekend, I was being inundated by phone messages from a guy repeatedly calling me when I was clearly not available. His final message was, "Thanks a lot for getting back to me (sarcasm added); I thought you were my psychologist." I shook my head when I heard that. "Your psychologist?" I thought, "No, pal, I was trying to be your friend."

Sometimes the closest connection that can be hoped for in a male friend is one which, in some circles, goes by the title of 'wingman.' A wingman has your best interests at heart. If you are single, he helps promote your cause to other, would-be-eligible others. If you are in a committed relationship, there is also the sense of being able to rely on each other for talks about love or work-related topics that bring you down. Usually, the moments of connection also entail some form of accompanying distraction, such as drinking, sarcastic humor, or just not lingering in a tough place too long. All of these act as buffers against the awkwardness of true moments of vulnerability and closeness. Given that these same men struggle to achieve proficiency in the skillset of intimacy with their wives and children, it's no surprise that this is also seen with friends, where many exchanges that could be so much more end up being a mixed experience. Even if your wingman really is not that accomplished in these delicate areas, you know he means well, and sometimes that is enough.

There is a long and complicated trial period between male friends, which can include a lot of male posturing, uncertainty about being too close, and the reviving of dings from previous male buddy connections that crashed and burned. Underlying these complications are unmet needs that are sometimes traced back to the formative years – such as dads who were not present, emotionally or physically. Honestly, all this is a lot to work through if you're a middle-aged male in the market for a new best friend.

I know I am not blameless, sometimes wandering alone in the desert in search of a new male wingman or compadre. I am not by nature a people person. I have my own social awkwardness, and have received the feedback that I can come across as aloof or uninterested. I also can be rigid in my level of expectations. If I give this much, so should you. All this being said, it is easier for me to be a support/mentor-like figure to other men. It is my way of safely connecting. I know what to expect and don't have to put myself out there. It is my job to just listen. My vulnerability is more apparent when I am on a level playing field with a potential friend. I cannot hide behind the shield of supporting someone. I have to bring myself to the table, and wade through the frustrations that go with any type of real connection, asking for what I need; owning up to the fact that I actually *do* need. All of this makes it much easier to attend regular meetings of men's group where I listen, and, in a strange sort of way, feel heard.

The Island of Misfit Toys

Another thing I remember vividly as a kid were the Christmas TV specials, which I watched with great devotion. There was *Frosty, the Grinch*, the *Peanuts* gang, and many others. My brother and I would be on the lookout for these shows airing shortly after Thanksgiving, and it would always be a friendly competition about who saw them advertised first.

My favorite of these shows was *Rudolph, the Red-Nosed Reindeer*. There was Rudolph with the glowing red nose, along with his vocationally challenged sidekick, Hermey the elf, who wanted to be a dentist. Neither character really did not fit into their assigned groups – they were misfits – and, after deciding that their present situations would not allow them to be who they really were, they set off on a journey to find more hospitable digs. On the way they meet Yukon Cornelius, the trapper, who searched for silver and gold.

Rudolph and his friends even extended their adventures to the Island of Misfit Toys, the rather melancholy place for toys that had never known the love of a child – their existential purpose in life. There was the train with square wheels, a cowboy who rode an ostrich, and a water gun that squirted jelly. Each year these three waited for Santa to gather them up from the island and deliver them to kids. Each year came and went, but no Santa. This part of the show must have made quite an impression on my brother and me, as we knew these lines by heart, though we delivered them with more of a comedic edge in order to create some distance from such a serious topic, about which we both resonated.

The story ends on a happily-ever-after note, as Rudolph finds his place leading Santa's sleigh, Hermey becomes a dentist to the elves, and the misfit toys finally get gathered up by Santa and delivered to kids around the world. I wondered, in the way that only a child can, "Will I be getting one of those misfit toys for Christmas this year?" It was a mix of curiosity and sympathy, "It would be okay to have a toy like that." It didn't matter much that they couldn't perform the duties that fate had dictated for them. After all, they seemed nice enough.

My brother and I loved to watch this show, and would have the sense of being cheated in the deepest possible way if somehow we missed it. Tuning in gave us a special feeling that was absent the rest of the year in our house. Rudolph and his friends also allowed my brother and me to sidestep some of the male bonding issues previously discussed. As adults reminiscing about growing up, neither of us could pretend that we were unaffected by our misfit status as children.

The thing that I did not realize until well into adulthood was the degree to which my own parents were misfits. At some point it dawned on me with great clarity that they were people with their own hopes and dreams of finding a place to belong. A place they hoped for, but had limited success in finding. What ensued for them only offered temporary respite. This said, as a child I didn't understand these things about my parents. It seemed strange that no one ever came to visit at the house besides extended family members. It is a daunting task for misfits, even with the best intent, to raise 'normal' kids without also passing on some of their own pain. What is felt with a thud is the emotional residual that can appear in the form of chronic loneliness.

Psychoanalyst Melanie Klein discussed the etiology of chronic loneliness. This should be understood differently from the temporary feeling of being lonely that is normal and everyone experiences. Klein argued that the enduring version is the result of an alienation from our sense of self.[5] This is a rather sophisticated way of saying that what has been experienced is too painful to stay connected with. The pain could be the result of childhood trauma, unbearable letdowns, or any of the events carrying the potential of imparting the label of misfit on its bearer. The problem with the painful personal history is made worse when these events actually form the central pillars of our personal narrative and identity. If one cannot have a relationship with these key elements, then there is little possibility of being warmed by the presence of others, even when they are interested and available.

Misfits come in all ages, shapes, and sizes. The men that I know fitting this category readily slide into a more lasting sense of loneliness. After all, the way males are taught to organize their sense of self is centrally based on one's notion of being a man; a definition that can easily take on misfit status. A man's sense of masculinity is also omnipresent, and is part and parcel of everything that is done and said. When I try to explain this gender-specific construction to those unfamiliar with it, it naturally seems strange that one aspect can be attached to so much territory, and can potentially dominate it all. Even when I do not say it directly, I am writing about it, and it is present here with every keystroke. Sometimes it is in the foreground of our being when addressing 'what it means to be a man' by name, and then in the background, when feeling touchy about seemingly unrelated topics, such as asking for directions and failing to maintain my lawn (both of which seem to be an unspoken violation of traditional male norms). In either case, 'being a man' is tied to each and every role and task.

If one's sense of masculinity is in healthy shape, that is good news, as its pervasive nature means maleness becomes a resource in all other areas in one's life. If, on the other hand, if it is chock-full of doubts and bruises from the formative years, it carries the potential of causing a male misfit to confront insecurities at each and every activity. Not only is that a taxing endeavor to negotiate, it also leaves doubts about one's worth.

A much older colleague shared with me his story of growing up as a misfit. In spite of this, he became highly successful, and his former schools invited him back to receive numerous awards for his many accomplishments. At each ceremony, though, he felt bewildered about why they were recognizing him, and could not understand why those in the audience, or the person presenting the award, could see him as anything other than a misfit. With all he had done, still some part of him questioned his legitimacy. He was also someone who loved his animal companions, once shyly sharing a poem about his most recent friend who had passed away. Like so many of us, when his canine companion was present, some of the static about being a man faded into the background for a few moments.

The American Adam begins sinking into chronic loneliness through a process that begins from the inside. Events which are connected to being a masculine misfit build one on top of another, and slowly lead him to a place beyond the reach of others. Friends, family, and significant others, not realizing what is going on, unwittingly see the solution as trying to engage him more, or help him find a hobby so he will not seem so alone. However, the real task is that he must face the necessary hurt in order to sort things out, and help the wayward parts of himself come back on line. This is best done with a companion who passes the safe-enough litmus test.

Understandably, some men do not find this option, or else decide it is easier to fake a smile and a handshake when in the company of others. It is one of the reasons I find it a necessary but difficult task facing what I feel; however, doing so acts as a tool, reminding me I am an active player in the choices affecting my life now. It prompts me to redefine what it means to be a man in each of the roles I assume: father, husband, friend, and a person touched deeply by the human-animal bond. It also opens me up to others and what they have gone through, becoming an instrument of connection with other misfits.

Adam's sidekick

Some men try to rise above the errors and limitations found within male socialization. I see such a scenario played out often in my work as a psychologist, and I know it personally as a man. Men who received the status quo set of rules governing manhood attempt to become retrained with another, more updated and relationship-friendly set of skills, which includes an attempt at doing a better job of bonding and sustaining ties. While the new point of view is less cluttered with mistakes, it does not guarantee a conflict-free existence.

In fact, realizing our true calling as sons of Adam who are capable of connecting can still be a frustrating journey, not to mention go against the grain of all that we have been taught as men.

With the updates and patches for the traditional masculine software, many stumble around trying to offset some of the relationship experiences missed out on or messed up along the way. But even when some movement is achieved, and some semblance of a social network set in place, there is still a yearning for a different type of encounter, and it is often at a juncture in the road marked by confusion and disappointment that a would-be animal companion first comes into view.

The presence of an animal companion has the potential to rekindle a hardwired part of us that still exists, buried deep below the challenges of masculine exceptionalism. Initially for some, the typical rules that govern men are still at play, and there is no guarantee that even a friendly tail wag will disarm or circumvent masculinity's impact on bonding. In fact, some may be very suspicious initially of such a welcoming character. "Go away!" some men may say, "Go far away ..."

Then something happens that is hard to define. Perhaps it is the steady presence, or the sense of being unwittingly lulled away from the self-isolating protection that most Adams have learned to depend on, but, to their credit and our betterment, our canine friend does not live in the same rule-bound and confusing world. Different guidelines apply, some of which make man and dog a natural and easy fit from the onset. Even if there is hesitation to release well-worn defenses, our canine companion seems willing to go where others fear to tread, over and over again, until the message is driven home that our connection really is true. There is the realization that it is okay to slowly begin removing our body armor, an intricate outer shell forged one section at a time; each piece the product of lessons learned over the long history of becoming a man. The suit of metal is handed down from one generation of Adams to the next, with each new occupant adding his own signature layers of protection. It does a fine job of keeping a man safe from external foes, real and imagined, but it does a horrible job of letting others near. For most men, the chest plate comes off last, as it protects the most vulnerable area he has learned to guard so well. But, once removed, a dog reaches deep inside the heart, taking hold in a way we always hoped somebody would.

One day like any other, I came home and sat down to take off my boots. Immediately, everything felt off. I was frustrated with my new job, felt alone after the ending of a taxing, long-term relationship, and, worst of all, Kelsey had recently passed away. The psychological body armor that was part of my everyday existence had doubled in thickness. On this occasion, Sadie, who was still young enough to be considered a puppy, seemed particularly interested in my feet, drawing close, pushing her nose against and tugging at my socks. I initially thought she was displaying playful pup behavior, and was going to make a new game by either biting my toes or socks. Instead, she plopped down on the floor and, with earnest devotion, began licking the soles of my feet. This sandpapering went on for a few minutes. I felt like I was in a National Geographic film being groomed in a caring way, one designed to lift me up and out of the dreary place I was in. Since that day, friends and family have heard about Sadie's compassionate act, and will try to entice the same treatment from her by waving their toes in the air as they sit on the sofa or a chair. Her usual response is to ignore such pandering, or, out of a sense of duty, confirm through a quick inspection that the feet on display are not mine, and then move on.

Sadie makes it a regular practice to enact the ritual of care, especially if I have been out of town for a few days. It also seems to occur when it has been a particularly trying day on my part. There have been times when I am too distracted to notice what she is attempting, but Sadie is not one to give up that easily. At first, she will gently nudge against my feet with the point of her nose. If I am not paying attention, she will increase her efforts until she is making a prodding motion that could easily tip over a man, or rival a dolphin's ability to cripple a shark. In these moments, it does not matter where I have been, or if my efforts elsewhere have left me with the distinct impression of being a misfit: I am welcomed home in a way that makes me feel like a successful man.

Social creatures

One of the truly life-changing aspects of my training in graduate school was discovering approaches to psychology which argue that human beings are literally hardwired to make and sustain connections with others. By nature, all humans – even men – are social creatures. One perspective that subscribes to this viewpoint was discussed previously. Attachment theory was inspired in part by the work of primate researcher Harry Harlow, who pioneered the 'mother love' studies in the 1960s.[6] Harlow showed the fierce and lasting bond among orphaned infant rhesus monkeys and their surrogate – inanimate, terry-cloth monkey mothers, constructed from wire covered by soft fabric. The infant monkeys would cling to their new 'moms' for up to sixteen hours a day, under all types of novel and adverse conditions concocted to separate them. They would even carry around bits of their 'mom' that came loose. At the time, the psychology community began wondering if animal studies that concerned bonding could have some implications for the human mother-child attachment as well. Some thought human babies, trying to establish an emotional tie, would react in similar ways with their mothers.

British psychoanalyst John Bowlby, the father of attachment theory, who operated at a time before the advent of daytime talk shows and personal confession booths on reality programs, began exploring the bond between human mother and child based on a need for bonding, a topic whose importance seems common knowledge today, but which, oddly, was not realized in psychology during the first fifty years. It was widely held that infants sought connection with parents, because it reduced their innate biological tensions. In essence, if you feed me or gratify me, I will love you. Instead, Bowlby suggested a more hardwired need for connection for its own sake.[7]

Without a bond, a child is in danger of becoming an asocial shell, or, even worse, literally perishing from the lack of contact. The fundamental connections are sought for far more than just someone to satisfy our wants and wishes in an impersonal manner. Having a well-met companion join us on life's journey brings meaning and richness.

At the time when I was first exposed to these perspectives in my training as a psychologist in the 1990s, I remember being simultaneously intrigued and confused. After all, the core message of needing someone for its own sake was in direct opposition to everything I knew about being a man, and a departure from some of the things I had learned within my own family.

There are some families that are so close they know each other's every move, feeling each small triumph or tragedy. Then there are those, similar to mine, that seemed to derive most of our relatedness from a shared address. This level of distance appeared to promote competition for all of the available resources, and the inability to be truly happy for someone else's happiness, because it seemed to have direct implications for short-changing your own. Very little was given freely in my family; instead, there were implied contracts and stipulations to be ironed out and enforced, sometimes even without knowing it.

I have been working since I was twelve years old. While that comment may lead you to liken it to something from a Charles Dickens novel, my family did not have a lot of resources. I picked up odd jobs, and my summers were spent mowing a lot of lawns (I pushed the lawnmower around our neighborhood from customer to customer, usually spanning a couple of miles). One hot July morning, I had just finished a lawn in less than ideal conditions. While all of my clientele were church-going folks, sometimes, they were a little light when it came time to pay the agreed upon price. "I will make up for it next time" or "Here, have a cookie instead" were common rejoinders. This was a big deal to a young entrepreneur whose main source of income came through these jobs, and whose family values were based on a skewed version of what money meant.

Having just gone through one of these episodes, I noticed that my mother had pulled into my client's drive. She instructed me to put the lawnmower in the back. "How nice, a ride home, this never happens," I thought, the kind gesture even providing some relief from being short-changed. We stopped unexpectedly in front of the corner convenience store. My mother turned to me and asked for her cut of my earnings for a snack. My surprised expression prompted the reply, "Well, I did something for you by giving you a ride, now you have to do something for me."

A few years later, when I had a summer construction job, my mother and I engaged in a tacit game of hide-and-seek. I hid my earnings and she found them. All the while I wondered if this was really happening, "Families don't really do these things to each other, do they?"

These stories reflect examples of a particular family theme, the shady version of quid pro quo, guiding a long and complicated series of exchanges involving what was owed and how debts were paid, and which continued for a long while. This theme strained relationships in my family and made giving and receiving an ugly experience.

Each of us had our own signature reactions. My mother would predictably develop a headache after the disappointment of opening Christmas presents and need to lie down. She would often call various family members in anxious desperation when money was short, and not come through when it came time to repay debts. My father had a preoccupation about being 'ripped off' by others, both in and outside of my family. At times, he also reminded me about all that he had done for me growing up, and offered various suggestions for how I could repay him after I finished school: "I think I would like a vintage Jaguar, not the four-door kind; the two-door

XKE convertible." (Price tag 60k.) Or, in my early thirties, when I was delinquent on delivering my father's Jaguar dream, but still had a little extra money after tax day, I spoke with him about a car. I was in the market for an old two-seater like the one I had in college, just more reliable. My father had one of these for sale, and called me up to make a deal, "Okay, well I listed it in the paper for four thousand, but for you I will go … five thousand." I think he meant it the other way around – that he would cut me a break on the price – but I still decided against the purchase.

I was reminded of my own version of give-and-take running into some friends I knew in graduate school who I had not seen in years. Back then, we would go to a Texas outdoor flea market: a square mile of antiques that often bordered on little more than junk-tiques. One of my friends reminisced, "Don't you remember … you had this whole routine about haggling while wearing your sunglasses so they couldn't see your eyes." In the moment, I uncomfortably winced, remembering. Yes, I had become a bargain hound, and the greatest victory was finding an unsuspecting dealer to exploit. At the time, I was not about to give anything away through the look of excitement in my eyes. This was just another version of watching out for my own best interests, and being leery of those who, no doubt, were only watching out for theirs. The cautious theme had filtered through my life in various ways; ones I would rather have left behind at that flea market long ago.

Some families pool their resources as a way to make ends meet. In the best situations, this approach can be a loving way to be a part of the family, or, for a boy, a way to show he is becoming a man by contributing. It can deepen household ties. However, in my family, what happened too often instead was a combination of a sucker punch following someone's warmth or kindness, which left me wondering whether any act of kindness could be taken at face value. These examples are not meant to imply that my parents were unkind; just that they felt cheated in their own lives, and tracking money and tangible goods were ways to take symbolical control of that.

However, the introduction of the idea of bonding for its own sake it meant being able to revise previously held views on what happened growing up, and why. Most do what we can to psychologically survive based on the premise that a connection is actually sought and needed, the reality of which is that sometimes desperate and awkward ploys are used in attempts to secure it. As in the case of my family, these strategies often backfired, and, instead of marshaling an esprit de corps, they drove others away. Holding a new perspective on these letdowns meant there was a chance that even old disappointments concerning give-and-take could begin to soften.

The new outlook also changed remnants of the dog-eat-dog approach in my own life. If I was hardwired to make and sustain a connection, then the other person (or dog) was, too. This shifted from the old, familiar trying to get something for nothing, to a respect for the other and the other's needs. I felt a need to rush home and explain all of this to Kelsey, "Don't you see, we need each other, and we're in it together?!" This was a game-changer, especially considering how the skewed notions of family indebtedness joined with all the self-sufficient manly truisms I had learned, each a by-product of my own route to survival. Instead, with an updated perspective, even men can learn to embrace being a social creature.

These are reasons why the next two topics are so important in the context of the human-animal bond.

Accompaniment

My curiosity about dog people also being social creatures was piqued by my training on psychological tests known as 'projectives.' As any introduction to psychology textbook will say, these are intended as the means of assessing the unconscious realm of the psyche. Someone may tell a story based upon a card that might have inkblots, or some cartoon-like still images, on them. While the cards can cause a great deal of anxiety when trying to construct a story, they actually have no intrinsic power themselves, and are merely a blank screen on which to project worries, preoccupations, and conflicts. When an examiner hands a card to the poor, unsuspecting person, and asks "What might this be?" or "Tell me a story about this card," a window is opened into that individual's inner world. Over the course of looking at and responding to numerous cards, a profile that describes how the individual sees the world, relationships, and themselves slowly emerges.

For those examinees who find human companionship daunting, there is a tendency to see all types of creatures, great and small, but very little 'human' content; people are generally missing from the scenes and stories they tell. One supervisor told me that a lack of humans implied that the subject was not quite prepared for social contact. I always found that interpretation a little disconcerting, since I was also one of those who saw lots of animals in the cards, but very few people!

One of the assumptions about those with special ties with animal companions is that they are all misanthropes, who missed out on the chance to make and sustain bonds with others. This carries a heavy pronouncement, like never being able to become a fully-functioning social creature. However, an ever-increasing focus about animal companions now exists among other curious minds and researchers from different fields who see the value of the bond in its own right. This includes fiction writers, mental health professionals, veterinarians, and filmmakers. Documentaries feature the rehabilitation of inmates through training dogs, and studies highlight how the presence of animal companions offset chronic emotional and physical effects. There are even therapy dogs in nursing homes. In a general sense, animal companions have a strong positive impact on human beings, and there is a growing wealth of empirical research suggesting they can influence health and well-being, combat stress and loneliness, and even aid in recovery from illness and operations.[8]

For some, animal companions are a forerunner to different types of social connections, while others enjoy the bond amid an already fulfilling social network. It is not an either/or situation when it comes to bonding: there are more complex and nuanced aspects to consider. Some research suggests that the choice of a canine companion is guided – at least in part – by how similar they are to us:[9] a dog with similar physical qualities: the same type of moustache, hairdo, or personal disposition, say. This same longing for a like-minded friend can also apply to unique emotional or physical history. Cheering for a dog who has had a tough time of it can feel, in some way, like rooting for a part of ourselves. In my own life, I often experienced a sense of impermanence with people, leading to a reluctance to focus on them. In the midst of roaming from place to place, the connection that remained constant throughout the fourteen years of my early adulthood was Kelsey. She was a continual presence, providing the experience of accompaniment.

While inanimate objects such as cars, shoes, or cell phones may be counted on in our daily lives, becoming much like Harlow's terry-cloth monkey moms, an animate being is really needed to accompany us on life's journey.

Accompaniment (or the experience of company) is necessary on both the small and grand scale, and includes big transitions, like relationship successes and failures, as well as the small moments that build, giving way to one quiet, but impactful realization that having someone present for life's day-to-day events fulfills a deep need. Each of us needs an eyewitness to give our life purpose and texture, and even confirm that the events actually have meaning. There is something psychologically grounding about the level of predictability associated with knowing that someone is there. It doesn't mean that they have to be perfect; nor does it imply that every moment is a celebration. It simply suggests that, in a world which can feel full of chaos, change, and impermanence, a steady, even presence that can always be counted on is remarkable. It is an anchor in the midst of the storm.

The cards containing inkblots and cartoon images known as projectives tell us something about how dog people, just like any other kind of people, need someone in their lives, but does not mean that animal companions are there just for 'practice,' in the hope that one can move on exclusively to human companions. There is something distinct and powerful about our bond, even when life is filled with satisfying relationships with human companions. Some argue that being with our animal companions makes us more human. I often suppose that it might be more accurate to say that our shared experiences actually allow us to become more capable social creatures. Our various bonds with human and animal companions allow us to attach to others in new and different ways; ones we may never have thought possible.

Attunement

Whereas accompaniment involves the constant presence of another, attunement is more specifically to do with when a companion recognizes and responds in sync to our current state of being. This is especially important on bad days when everything goes wrong, but is also needed over the course of many life events, from triumph to tragedy. Recent research suggests that dogs possess a unique ability to clearly discriminate between human emotions, and then respond in kind, even to the point of predicting what will come next.[10] This can include reacting to our changes in mood (good or bad), and physical well-being. For example, a canine companion becomes a 'Velcro dog' for migraine sufferers, lying by their owner's side, or just staring intently, at the onset of a headache. While there might be a temptation to feature your dog on a psychic hotline, the real magic is based on the ability to recognize very subtle facial cues, which canine companions have mastered over the estimated 15,000 years that man and dog have spent together.[11] Needless to say, that is a successful long-term relationship by any standards.

Cognitive scientist Alexandra Hortwitz, PhD points out that dogs and primates are unique in the non-human animal kingdom in their ability to offer a mutual gaze.[12] That is, human and dog look at each other in a sustained way, registering facial expressions. Other research goes further, suggesting that dogs even outshine man's closest genetic cousin in the 'left-gaze bias.'[13] When a dog looks at a human face, this includes scanning the right side of the face (which is actually the left side from the dog's perspective) for telltale signs of emotional cues. Until recently, it was thought that only humans showed this type of gaze-bias, given that the human face is lopsided in exhibiting micro expressions related to displaying emotions: the left side (from the observer's perspective) gives much more unfiltered information about how we feel.

In controlled lab experiments, dogs are fitted with special headgear which allows tracking of their eye movements as they view various pictures. Dogs will intuitively show the left-gaze bias for photos of human faces, which does not occur when watching other animals or inanimate objects. It can be argued that the left-gaze bias is particularly important for tracking emotion, and then offering a sense of attunement. When expressing emotions, especially strong ones, this is not lost on our canine companions. A tail wag, jump in your lap, well-placed bark, or even hunkering down beside you at the right moment, are all real acts of support. When the verbal or non-verbal communication is in-tune between two parties, it creates the psychological experience of having been heard, having another being attuned with one's needs.

Attunement is argued by

many in psychology to be among the most quintessential of human needs.[14] It is good to have others present – and even react to us – but it is best when they respond by being in-step with us in the moment. This includes having someone be attuned across a wide array of emotional responses. Attunement has direct implications for a variety of settings, including being a model for how a caregiver interacts with his or her children. A child's self-awareness and sense of self are enhanced by the right level of attunement. While attunement has been a particular focus for the health and welfare of infants and children, this same concept is important for adults. Attunement is a necessary part of vibrant adult interactions which range from good friends and romantic partners to the healing power of the therapeutic relationship. In terms of the latter, psychoanalyst Heniz Kohut suggested that one aspect of attunement, empathy – or the ability to know the inner world of another – was the major tool of psychoanalysis.[15] While that may conjure up images of a Freud-like canine companion sporting a goatee, fully equipped with a leather couch, there is not doubt that dogs add a unique healing presence in many of our lives.

Alone together

The potential benefits of accompaniment and attunement include facilitating another's self-exploration and growth, deepening the sense of emotional bonding within a connection, and even healing from pain in our past. These key characteristics also play another role: knowing when to give others a healthy sense of psychological 'space.'

Psychoanalyst Donald Winnicott argued that 'me-time' is a necessary aspect of our own ongoing maintenance and well-being.[16] Everyone has their own version of what this looks like – reading the paper, a quiet walk – and one of my favorites: starting each day with a cup of coffee in my favorite chair by a window looking into the garden. In these moments of comfortable solitude, any out-of-sync intrusions crashing into our needed space are absent. Me-time provides an opportunity to allow what is being learned or experienced about the world, relationships, and ourselves to sink in, finding their proper place. It is a restorative occurrence, allowing for psychological evenness. Winnicott suggested that the disruptive occurrence of having someone encroach into one's space at this vital juncture can be avoided if another is attuned enough to know when to keep a safe distance. Winnicott was also careful to say that this is not a choice between living in total isolation or being potentially overwhelmed by the company of others. Sometimes the practice of dialing into one's own experience can occur in the company of another, or what he describes as 'being alone with others.' That is, our alone time occurs within a shared space with someone who is also exploring his/her own me-time. Common examples include reading the paper together, or being on a road trip where each person is doing their own thing, but in a shared area.

I think our relationships with animal companions also provide the much-needed experience of being alone with others. It is also a prime way that men learn to compensate for some of the adverse effects of male socialization, a phenomenon often full of misattunement. When some of our prior bonding experiences have left us feeling somewhat uncomfortable in a direct, no shields up way of connecting, sharing the space with another who is in sync allows for a corrective and much-needed encounter. Being alone together allows one to experience thoughts and feelings safely in the presence of someone else. When the occurrence becomes a relied-upon element within a relationship, it can produce the sense of having a witness to one's life, participating in its comings and goings in an attuned way.

For all of their importance, the art of listening and responding with accompaniment and attunement, and being alone together is no easy thing for many of us to acquire, much less expect as a normal part of our daily experience. This may be especially true in a modern world when the premium for these skills is often lost among the numerous interruptions occurring through multi-tasking, or over-reliance on social media to be seen and known by others (eg "I Tweet, therefore I am …"). These artificial formats fall far short of the aspects I am describing in this more intimate encounter between man and dog. However, the presence or absence of these qualities shape our very essence.

There are many times when Sadie and I directly engage with each other through play, offering a treat, or combing her coat that sheds so much, which I am sure could produce a few sweaters. In other moments, especially on our twice-a-day walks, we provide each other with a sense of being alone together. I use our walks as a way of sorting through the remains of the day, often in regards to my work, and Sadie seems to use them as a way of catching up on the latest smells left on the path that we frequent. We attune to each other's rhythm, pausing here and there based upon one another's needs. There occurs a sort of dance, Sadie and I being both separate and together with each new step.

Living the dream

Looking across the history of the American Adam, it is true that he comes from different parts of the country, does different jobs, and even wears a diverse set of uniforms. There is, however, one constant truth for all of them: all of the Adams need at least one reliable connection, and are enhanced by the presence of many healthy ones. The source of those connections can involve human and non-human companions alike. While a bond is certainly important in the formative years, the need for an unfailing tie is a fixed part of human nature; something never outgrown. Even if much of male socialization argues to the contrary, being hardwired to attach to others is not a mark of immaturity or incompleteness, but rather a reflection of who men really are underneath the complex layers of being told what a man *should* be.

In the midst of the discovery process regarding how masculinity and connecting are actually compatible concepts, men strive to uncover the real truth – that a deep tie with another actually helps us come into our own, becoming a more complete version of ourselves. A strong bond does not limit vigorous masculinity, but instead helps each type of Adam realize a new version of masculine exceptionalism as the next step in the evolution of the American Dream; one marked by a willingness to share adventures with someone.

It is lucky for the misfit sons of the American Adam that some have dogs. I cannot speak to the mind of a canine companion with absolute certainty, but I feel in my heart that 'misfit' is not part of the dog lexicon for mankind. Or, if it is, it is a term applied with a wide berth of grace and understanding to all humans, and one that stirs sympathy rather than rebuff. When I have looked into Kelsey's and Sadie's eyes, what I see reflected back to me is the message, "Just because you can't see yourself with so much generosity doesn't mean I can't." Dogs have a healing presence, and have played a pivotal role in my own life. Due in large part to their care, I can reorient myself as a man who does seek connection with others, albeit in my own limited ways.

4

All good things are wild and free

"The soul is like a wild animal – tough, resilient, savvy, self-sufficient, and yet exceedingly shy. If we want to see a wild animal, the last thing we should do is go crashing through the woods, shouting for the creature to come out. But if we are willing to walk quietly into the woods, and sit silently for an hour or two at the base of the tree, the creature we are waiting for may well emerge, and out of the corner of an eye we will catch a glimpse of the precious wildness we seek."
– Parker Palmer, *The Broken Open-Heart*

There is a special place not far from my house where Sadie and I walk. If our timing is right, we see the 'Monarch of the Glen,' my nickname for a magical creature who inhabits the forest. Part of his distinct appearance is a more-than-twelve-point rack of antlers standing three feet from his head. He has a triangular beard, and his eyes are ancient and regal.

The first time I saw this deer, I could not help but nod my head in admiration, and each time I subsequently encounter the Monarch, it stirs another reaction – wonder. I am drawn out of my normal experience of time and space: my heart rate slows, and my body relaxes. What, initially, was an experience of watching another creature changes; I now feel like I have joined with him, both of us small parts of something bigger. Sadie also seems strangely calm,

and does not attempt to cross over into the tree line where he always stands.

I have never seen the Monarch out in the open. A thin veil of shrubs or a low-lying tree marks the entrance to his realm, one that, for a few moments, is approached. We stand there taking each other in, and when it is time to part ways, I pay my respects. As I walk away, I realize I am affected by this experience. It lingers. I feel gentle, wild, and alive.

On another day at dusk, Sadie and I come across one of the Monarch's great-grandsons. Sadie picks up the scent, and we round the corner of a trail that opens into a small clearing. There is a proud buck with does of various ages in his family. He seems somewhat surprised to see us. Stillness gives way to movement, and the buck stomps and snorts. The cold air makes his breath visible, which takes the shape of a cloud that hangs around his face. Sadie begins to pull, wanting off the lead.

After what seems like an eternity, the deer suddenly bolt. Most go directly into the woods, but the buck puts on a special show, running in the other direction and jumping high in the air, easily clearing the brush. As he hovers between the earth and sky, it is as though the laws of gravity have been temporarily suspended. Sadie wants to chase the Monarch's kin. I have no concern that she will catch him, or that the chase will go on for very long, so I let her run free. Before I know it, I also feel something primal inside me, my pulse quickens, and my life has a singular purpose in that moment. I suddenly find myself moving through the woods, following, struggling to keep up. I do not wish to hunt the deer, hoping only that he will let me share the wildness. I want to experience what seems to be a natural state of being; one unfettered by the constraints I too often feel.

The qualities I am trying to describe are derived from encounters with 'the wild.' This is not an easy concept to define. In fact, as mountain guide/ philosopher Jack Turner argues in his book, *The Abstract Wild*, modern culture is so removed from a firsthand encounter that the wild has already become an abstract concept for many.[1] Henry David Thoreau believed that wildness (the 'animal in us') was among man's most valuable assets, and reminds us that "… all good things are wild and free."[2] For Thoreau, wildness was present in many different things – literature, religious texts, mythology – and, of course, nature. Thoreau argued that wildness is the source of vitality, creativity, and strength, the essential "raw-material of life." Sustained growth at individual or cultural levels is determined by a connection with this primal energy. Likewise, if contact is lost with wildness, dullness and weakness set in.

I agree that wildness can be found in many different forms; it can be both gentle and fierce. Our connection with it can be established through our surroundings – like being in nature – and even through deeply held feelings that stir inspiration from within. Sometimes, wildness compels stillness and contemplation; other times, it strikes like a lightning bolt, prompting immediate action. Being wild is an essential quality. All the best manifestations eventually lead to the same experience: a feeling of being alive. The importance of such a sensation cannot be underestimated as a human necessity, but it assumes its own unique meaning in the lives of men.

While Thoreau remarked that all good things are wild and free, the North American male tends to be further separated from these qualities, weighed down by the impossible restrictions of what it means to be a man. By the time many reach middle age, the possibility of feeling alive has been replaced with numbness, or a dull ache that acts as a reminder of something which once stood in its place that had the possibility of being more vital. Some males at this stage of life acquiesce to the malaise, and become shells of who they once were, mechanically going through the motions in both work and love. Others go to great lengths to try and capture an encounter with the elusive quality of wildness in what becomes the 'age of toys,' where grown men seek out the next wild thing that money affords; some momentary escape from the clutches of the deadening that has firmly taken hold inside. Maybe the great escape takes the form of a motorcycle, or a vintage muscle car. Sometimes, wildness is also pursued through an out-of-the-ordinary experience, like running with the bulls, or a flirtation with someone half our age. Obviously, not all forms of wildness are part of a long-term solution, or are in our best interests, but each is an attempt to engage in the spirit of what Freud called the 'life instinct': an innate need to preserve life and create it.[3] A tiny drop of this magic water has the potential of allowing at least a temporary return to the land of the living.

In the last quarter century or so, there has been a growing abundance of research connecting the influence of animal companions in our everyday lives to health. Early research by Erika Friedmann. Alan Beck and Arron Katcher showed how the bond was related to improved cardiac surgery recovery and decreased mortality.[4] It has subsequently also been connected to improvement in a number of chronic and short-term illnesses. Beyond findings affectiing our physical health, there are also ones that link to mental health.[5]

The presence of animal friends in one's life is associated with elevated positive moods, a sense of belonging and companionship, all of which – as social animals searching for emotional bonds – we need. The generative effects may be especially important for at-risk populations that experience chronic loneliness, have trouble making or sustaining connections with others, and are going through major life transitions, such as divorce or job loss. They also have direct implications for those who have lost touch with a sense of the wild.

Men's animal companions are a conduit to wildness. Their presence helps satisfy the archetypal quest to feel alive. The bond becomes a tonic that has the potential to brace mankind, even amid all of the confusing trappings of modernity and problems with masculinity. In this chapter, it is revealed how animal companions play a pivotal role in keeping the embers of the wild fire burning within.

Wildness makes us whole

Struggling to find a place within us for wildness is a topic I have often come across in my own clinical practice working with men. Truth be told, it is something I know about firsthand, as well. It is easy to be confused about what it means to be wild at heart: for some, it seems like only a small, dangerous step away from a killer ape running amok, bent on gratifying needs with little or no consideration for others. If this is the sum total of one's relationship with the wild, then it has become a spoiled asset, only representing a severely skewed version of how it can influence a man's life. It takes work to find a lasting connection with wildness.

Some of my earliest and most conflicted notions of wildness were shaped by and took hold in my youth. One influence was being raised to attend the weekly double-header of Sunday school and church. As Methodists, we were both devout and mild, cherishing each new opportunity to turn the other cheek. Another somewhat contrasting image was the less-than-saint-like happenings in my school and neighborhood, where fights regularly broke out on playgrounds, at bus stops, and on any occasions when a boy's notion of pride and honor were at stake. The act of fighting was part of the working-class notion of being tough enough and man enough. Aggression is a form of wildness that is often misunderstood, and seen only as an out-of-control force.

My first real fight happened with the neighbor down the street when I was five years old. What I remember most is an exchange of insults and ultimatums as we got off the bus at the end of the school day. Some of that really triggered me, because I remember a switch being flipped in my head and, with it, an angry lunge at the other boy. As older kids pulled me off him, and I began returning from a state of rage I never knew I had, I began wondering why I was trying to pummel his already-bloody lip and nose. Why did I feel scared, guilty, and even a little like crying as I walked home half a block to my house? After the initial incident, my neighbor and I enacted a similar ritual, exchanging blows about every six months or so. We were never close friends, and when we tried to hang out for any extended period of time, we usually ended up brawling.

I look back now, trying to make sense of who I was as a boy. I think an overly constrained appearance left many with the sense that I was a nice, but burdened, kid. When prompted, I sat in the classroom with my arms on the top of my desk, fingers interlaced, just like my first-grade teacher taught me. I learned that this was the posture assumed by all well-behaved young men in school. The nuance to complete the scene was how tightly I held my hands together, like a sort of twisted prayer being offered in hopes of lightening the load that fell squarely upon my shoulders. Some of it concerned how to express my natural wild inclinations: a topic I had yet to come to grips with. There was also the expression of out-of-control pseudo-wildness manufactured by the stress in my family, where things felt beyond my ability to manage or control. For a long time, I thought true natural wildness and the version born from frustration, disappointment, or needing someone to be the target of blame were one and the same. This point of confusion locked the doors and made all versions of wildness seem off-limits. When one form did show up, it got peppered by the other and went too far. I needed some way to work out the contrasting wild parts of me. My early efforts to do so included playing sports.

I was not a gifted athlete. I was one of your 'play from the heart' players who, when something was lit inside, could move past the layers of restraint that normal living imposed. That something usually involved the familiar themes, like getting angry, feeling shamed, or some kind of righteous indignation that even Methodists might agree warranted opening up on someone. I was also probably more naïve than most, believing the sporting world was primarily about shaping young men's lives, and most – if not all coaches – saw this as their task. No doubt there were some who did, and I had the opportunity to know a few, but, by and large, I left high school with an impression of the opposite.

I played football each fall beginning in the third grade. During my sophomore year in high school, I started on the varsity team a few times under the guidance of a philosopher-coach who I much admired. Upon his retirement, I had much more direct interaction with Coach M, however, who became a character within a dream sequence stretching out for the next twenty years. The dreams always accompanied the change of seasons marking the beginning of football season. Coach M had briefly played professional football, but a serious knee injury cut short his career. He was still young enough to remember his glory years, but not quite seasoned enough to keep his intensity in check. He wanted to win more than anyone I had ever met. If he could not accomplish this by being on the field, he would do so by pushing

his team to victory. When the score was not in our favor, it was not safe to be on the front bench in the locker room. As we headed in for half-time, the message was passed from one anxious adolescent boy to another, "We should keep our helmets on."

The dreams with coach usually involved him keeping me on the sidelines, even when I wanted more than anything to prove myself. I felt a level of silent frustration rise sharply inside, triggering me to wake up. Maybe if I was able to stay in the dream longer, I would find a clumsy way of advocating on my own behalf. The thing I was most afraid of was tapping into the anger that might also unhinge me, disturbing the not-so-gentle balance that kept wildness in check. Giving into that felt like breaking a set of deeply held rules, by far the greater of two evils.

After many cycles and much personal work on wildness, the last dream I had of him was different. I was on the sideline again, but this time the coach and I had aged. I saw him as a frustrated and somewhat frail older man who struggled to keep command of his players and himself. He aroused my sympathy more than my ire. With a kindly invitation to enter the game and a successful tackle that followed, I realized that there was no need to continue being on this playing field: it was not where I belonged any more.

It would be easy to mistake the coach in my dreams as only one person, when, in reality, he is actually a composite of pivotal players who taught me about an

All good things are wild and free

edgy, unbridled form of wildness that was then filtered through my own personal liabilities. The main players in the dreams, a boy and a coach, are also ultimately different sides of me trying to find workable relationships with something I did not fully understand.

In real life I did not play football during my senior in high school. I recall the conversation I had with Coach M, telling him I would not be returning the next season. He tried to persuade me otherwise, arguing I would see a lot of playing time, but I had made up my mind. On one hand, the decision led to an understandable sense of incompleteness: I was lacking the capstone event for something I had invested a significant amount of time and energy in. At first, it seemed this was the reason the dreams would appear each fall, but something more needed sorting out. I was working toward an understanding about how all boys and men struggle with what to do with our wild side. We try to find tangible ways to approach it, comprehend it, and, if possible, befriend it.

It would be easy to assume that, with my pivotal breakthrough on the topic of wildness, it was taken care of, case closed. That would be an overestimation, as I have learned that it is a skill in need of perpetual fine-tuning. How much is effective? How much is too much? There is no one-size-fits-all ruler guiding every occasion.

Strangely enough, from time to time I find myself making an old familiar gesture: white-knuckled fingers interlaced and placed in front of me. In moments of self-awareness, I purposely unclench. My mind then wanders to recollections from my childhood that tell me I can still fight if I need to. It is not in the way that I did as a five-year-old stepping off the bus and into a state of blind rage. These days, the primal edge is felt in a different way. I try to court a reasonable relationship with restraint, which, in turn, makes it possible for more wildness to also be present. It does not have to be an either/or proposition of containing one and only allowing the other part of me to be present. If there was not a hint of wildness around me when I needed it, I would remain an incomplete person. This is where the bond between man and dog has the potential to offset some of the challenges.

The shadow sides of wildness

Wilfred is a TV show featuring Ryan, an overly nice but feckless man who, in his despair, has developed suicidal tendencies. He discovers a sort of life coach in the form of Wilfred, the dog. What is unique is that Ryan sees Wilfred as a man dressed in a canine costume, while everyone else sees him as a fully-fledged canine.

Wilfred is a character you may encounter in today's bromance films, in which bros help each other learn valuable life lessons about work and love. Also consistent with the bromance genre is the adage that opposites attract. While Ryan is meek and mild, Wilfred is a wild thing – barking, digging, humping, and willing to show his aggressive tendencies. Wilfred cajoles Ryan to stop cowering and stand up for himself. He identifies Ryan as one of the "good boys ... who always comes when he is called ..."

In the series opener, Wilfred takes his not-so-gentle blend of undomesticated behavior to a curious level. As a way of marking boundaries, and as part of a campaign against the terrorizing neighborhood bully, Wilfred and Ryan break into the oppressor's house. While there, Wilfred decides to empty his bowels in the bully's boot. When he finishes, Wilfred remarks to Ryan that there is still one boot left – an invitation to join the pack of wild ones with whom Ryan has clearly lost touch. Ryan's reaction, "I am not an animal!" prompts Wilfred to counter with, "Well, at least be a man, for once."

Imbedded within the exchange is a certain overstatement, but what is the take-home message? Who is actually wearing the costume: a dog posing as a man, or a man pretending not to be an animal? Will Ryan and those like him discover their inner wild animal, ready to throw off the shackles of over-domestication? Only time will tell.

One of the many reasons our canine friends have such an appeal is because they are a reminder of a disguised, if not forgotten, part of ourselves: a shadow side which men simultaneously wish and fear to know more about. Carl Jung developed the notion of the shadow, those aspects that remain disavowed or merely under-developed.[6] The shadow is usually not a dark or sinister part like Dr Jekyll's Mr Hyde; rather, it covers a broad range of attributes which,

when sorted through, are actually useful in our lives. Jung talked about the shadow-side being 90 percent golden, in the sense that coming to know and own it makes a person more complete. Without the shadow, a part of us is always missing.

There are so many different ways to pigeonhole or misread true wildness, some of which, understandably, lead to unease, being misinterpreted only in their most asocial ways. The true version of wildness is something far more substantial. Being wild can hold an element of danger, in part because it pushes one to be more open to life and engaging in an experience. Wildness helps one feel alive – a wild thing being allowed to run free. But, depending upon one's frame of reference, loosening the collar just a little can also court simultaneous reactions of freedom and fear, with the accompanying worry that it will always go too far. Keep in mind that being wild prizes the sanctity in each living element. A real relationship with wildness is never minted until a sense of responsibility and respect are also added to the pact.

There is a medieval story involving St Francis of Assisi and a wolf. St Francis was visiting the Italian town of Gubbio, where the townspeople reported that a wolf had been making threatening gestures. Francis met with the wolf and, being skilled with various members of the animal kingdom – as many of today's garden statuary and birdbaths can attest – came to an agreement. The contract provided that the villagers would feed the wolf daily, and allow him to wander freely among them. In exchange, the wolf agreed not to harm any humans or animals there.

The metaphor for feeding the wolf daily and allowing him to wander among the people speaks to the psychological task of coming to terms with our wildness. Barry Holsstrum Lopez interprets the story of St Francis of Assisi and the wolf as a medieval man trying to do just that in the context of the Dark Ages.[7] Animal symbolism is often used as a sign that a man is struggling with his wild nature. Likewise, the same approach is seen in more contemporary psychology as well. One of Freud's most famous patients was nicknamed the 'Wolfman.'[8] The Wolfman was the son of wealthy Russian landowners, who had acquired his aka status from a dream he'd had. In the dream, six white wolves sit high in the branches of a nearby walnut tree. The wolves, eerily motionless, have a dog-like appearance, and stare at the dreamer with ears pricked. The dreamer, fearing that he would be eaten, awoke in terror. Among other things, Freud interpreted that his patient was conflicted about his primal nature, concluding that the Wolfman had a "completely unbridled emotional life." The crux of why dogs, wolves, and the Wolfman are relevant among this discussion is because most men don't know what to do with their wildness. Instead it is banished, hunted down, and brought to heel, or, alternatively, is only known and expressed in an extreme version, with fangs and growls gone wild. Psychologically speaking, either case may present some problems.

Our shadow side is an invitation to allow the primal part of our nature to be exactly that, a part of our nature, not hidden, distorted, or unchecked. In exchange, it will begin to find its home. Thoreau suggested that wildness was at its best when held in its proper place by man's "higher nature." He said he lived "a sort of border life" between the civilized and the wild. This middle path allowed him to experience aspects of both ways of living. For many, a wild presence is needed as an inspiration, one that helps prompt the journey. When wildness becomes represented in tangible ways, it invites primal themes into our dreams or as a regular part of our lives. In the hour of the wolf, man meets the human-animal, and himself.

The call of the wild

Besides reliving old childhood battles, and breaking bad, there are other ways to hear the call of the wild. This is where animal companions come in, and can be of help to many men, both those who shun wildness and those who seek it. If part of what is seen in our dogs is a banished part of ourselves – that shadow side – then any and all co-adventures are really disguised attempts to reunite with a piece of ourselves that has gone missing. Wildness is not something that dogs put on and take off. Even if they know how to sit on command, their wildness is still always present. A dog is a Zen master, reminding us with each bark that part of our true nature lies hidden beneath convoluted grey matter, a facet of the brain that proves helpful in many situations, but can sometimes get in the way of a relationship with the wild.

Psychologist Boris Levinson is credited as the modern-day father of animal-assisted therapy, where animal companions assume a sort of co-therapist role in a variety of settings.[9] Their presence adds a unique dimension to the therapeutic encounter. Levinson began utilizing a therapy animal as a way for his patients to feel at ease, to be a source of soothing in difficult moments, and even provide a sort of social skills seminary regarding reading cues and setting interpersonal boundaries. Levinson explained the underlying reasons for the power of the therapeutic interactions occurring when his dog was present, suggesting that our sense of being connected to nature – and subsequently the wildness – is lost in modern times –

"One of the chief reasons for man's present difficulties is his inability to come to terms with his inner self and to harmonize his culture with his membership in the world of nature. Rational man has become alienated from himself by refusing to face his irrational self, his own past personified by animals."[10]

Levinson suggested that reconnection with nature could be had by establishing good relationships with animal companions. Animal companions become the "halfway station" on the road back to completeness. He argued that animals have played such a prominent role in our evolution, because humans also depend upon them in integral ways for our well-being. Animals are not only symbols of our unresolved conflicts or incompleteness, but also a part of the cure. We are made whole in the presence of their wildness.

Play

Play is another concept not easily defined, in part because, until recently, it was rarely studied in adults. Sometimes, playfulness is considered childish after a certain age, and, in the male world, can even be misunderstood as boyish or unmanly. Yet, this quality is essential in our lives. It is closely tied to wildness, providing spontaneity, creativity, and a different way of experiencing the world. In 1938, Dutch historian Johan Huizinga offered the following definition of play involving the notion of a "magic circle," where we experience "a separate and independent sphere of human activity"[11] –

"Summing up the formal characteristic of play, we might call it a free activity standing quite consciously outside 'ordinary' life as being 'not serious,' but, at the same time, absorbing the player intensely and utterly. It is an activity connected with no material interest, and no profit can be gained by it. It proceeds within its own proper boundaries of time and space according to fixed rules and in an orderly manner." – Johan Huizinga, *Homo Ludens* (Playing Man). It is important to note that Huizinga also makes it clear that animals knew how to play first –

"Play is older than culture,

for culture, however inadequately defined, always presupposes human society, and animals have not waited for man to teach them their playing."

Recent research trying to understand why animals play argues for its adaptive function.[12] The social play which most have witnessed in nature films becomes a means whereby pups and cubs try to hone abilities that will be of use later as an adult. This may comprise skills like hunting and fishing, but also includes how to make and sustain bonds. Play is crucial in order to be a successful adult: it allows the necessary relation skillsets to emerge. However, John Bradshaw suggests in *Dog Sense* that there may be other benefits –

"In wild animals, play must promote survival; otherwise, evolution would select against it – a young animal that is playing out in the open is much more obvious to a predator than one sleeping in its den. However, the benefits of play do not usually become apparent until months later, when they emerge in the form of better social integration or more sophisticated hunting techniques (to name but two, which vary from one species to another). Again, the simplest explanation is that play is self-rewarding: in other words – it is fun!"[13]

In a similar way, it has been suggested that, among human animals, play also helps the immature brain develop,[14] though, likewise, that is not the only benefit. Within the magic circle of playfulness, more serious attitudes are kept at bay. This includes those are all-too-familiar within the male world of sports: self-consciousness, embarrassment, or shame. No one likes to be picked last for a team, or be a part of the highlight reel for losing the game, shown hourly on SportsCenter. Instead, with our dogs there is the opportunity to enter a different frame of mind, one that allows the opportunity to be wild and free. Play at its best is a form of re-creation, reviving ourselves through a tie with wildness. Play is fun under most circumstances, but takes its wildest form when there is someone to share it with. Man's best friend helps here, as well. There may be the assumption among some that the human is the Alpha leader, but dogs are actually the ones guiding us into the realm of play. The limiting cultural definitions of masculinity are kept on the outside; this includes the notion that play is primarily about dominating someone, a power trip involving getting one-up on someone else. Instead, men go alongside our animal companions in the rain, find ourselves caught in an exhausting game of catch, or wrestle playfully for the right to call a chew toy our own. The thing is, there is no winning or losing when it comes to playing with our canine companions; there is just a sense of being caught up in the moment with a friend, the shared efforts creating a different type of reality.

Some of our play is ritualized, carried out first thing each morning, or a part of the winding down process after dinner at the end of the day, and some of it is spontaneous: new forms of play get created in the moment. Kelsey loved to howl. She could be prompted by a dog down the street, the sound of a distant train, or sometimes by the right note in the music I was listening to. She seemed so sincere about her efforts, head back, utterly devoted to producing a call of the wild, that I could not help but sometimes join in. Play in these moments takes on a different meaning in the context of men's lives. It becomes a way to connect – with each other, with what is inside us, and what is around us. It creates a psychological space where feelings that may seem off-limits elsewhere are allowed to emerge. The wild ones get unleashed. They move unfettered in our consciousness; their presence is soothing, allowing for reaching out and forming a bond. In a recent study, we found that men were able to significantly increase their levels of playfulness simply by calling on the memory of a playful time with their dog.[15]

Some dog trainers suggest that our animal companions need at least one daily walk to help sustain a pack mentality with their owners. From my way of seeing it, men need that same experience for not so different reasons. That is, these shared encounters help dial into a sense of mutual wildness. Our canine friends have their heads low to the ground, and rely on clever noses to commune with each flower and blade of grass. If men are smart, they do not actually *walk* their dogs, but instead *accompany* them on the journey. We make an effort to go alongside them, and when the wildness is unearthed, it brushes over us as well. In that moment, a different state of mind is entered, one that invites the experience of being whole. It has the power to cut through layers of usual, day-to-day mandates that separate us from ourselves based on what society says being a man means. In shared moments with our dogs, however, the constraining instructions which guide so much of our lives lose their power. Our bond with animal companions allows the possibility of simultaneously engaging external and internal sources of wildness. The animal inside us joins with the one on four legs leading the way.

These days, some of my best communicating with wildness occurs on daily adventures with Sadie. In some instances, I feel that we are explorers in a sometimes mysterious and hidden realm, even when stepping on the familiar tracks made the previous day in a local park. I have come to realize as of late that our exploits, even on inhospitable days, are as much for me as they are for her. If I were alone in the woods without Sadie, something would be missing. Her presence is necessary for the proper alignment with wildness. I feel things during our excursions that are unique, and not encountered throughout the rest of my day. I try to set aside time when I return from our escapades to write or work on a project, labeling it as my most productive time. It is a way to coax that special experience to stay with me for just a little longer.

Historical struggles for wildness

Ours is not the first generation attempting to court a reasonable relationship with wildness, in the realisation that something important is at risk of being lost. Turn back the clock a few hundred years and there are the 18th century Romantics and then the 19th century American Transcendentalists, both of whom were also involved in a very similar dialogue. Part of their motivation for doing so has a familiar ring: the worry about an ever-increasing mechanized world. Each sought nature as a counterbalance for the effect of modernity on the primal soul.

If nature and wildness are a remedy for modern ills, there is still a concern about how to find a regular communion with them. However, reading *Walden*, Henry David Thoreau's attempt to live deliberately in a little cabin in the woods for two years, two months, and two days, gives hope because his efforts to do so took place only a stone's throw from his family's home, where he returned regularly for supper and supplies.[16] Having a relationship with the wild does not necessarily entail taking up permanent residence on a secluded mountainside. Even modern man can commune with wildness. Given that the human-animal brain is still predisposed to respond to certain cues, there is a real possibility of learning to dial into that vital resource wherever he may be. But that takes effort, and a special commitment to break free from the relentless pursuit of being wired-in and multi-tasking faster than the speed of light. Even with that intent, many still need a friend to prompt the wildness to come alive. Our time spent with dogs is a contemporary anecdote

to the destabilizing effects of being piecemeal people, missing a vital part of our inherent birthright. It can be rediscovered in our own version of *Walden*, in the form of a dog park, a nearby creek, or even our own backyard.

For some, a powerful encounter may occur when various elements of the wild are brought together in one encounter – internal and external wildness. The presence of dogs and nature whirl together in a distinct tempo where many players meet, each adding something to the mix. I think back to another time many years ago when such a combination left its mark on me.

Follow the leader

My refuge during the years I spent in graduate school was a seasonal camp that my brother ran in Kansas. It was not the wheatfields or the homage to Dorothy and the Wizard of Oz that you might expect, but, instead, was a wooded site off the beaten track about seven miles from the nearest small town.

There were horses at the camp, about 40 mixed breeds and pedigrees. While I had been on a horse on a number of occasions, I learned to ride with the help of 'Sugar' – a reddish-colored, mixed-breed horse who had a taste for mischief. I recall Sugar and I bolting across a field of high grass, and it felt like something out of a movie where we moved in slow motion, frame by frame, except I was clinging to Sugar's mane, the saddle horn, and anything else I could find in the moment! She would sometimes run straight for a low-lying branch of a tree, or zoom at breakneck speed just inches from a fence. I had not learned to stay in the seat with any certainty yet, and Sugar knew it. Each ride seemed like a brush with certain death, but the simultaneously-experenced terror and thrill were exhilarating. In quieter moments, my brother and I would take trail rides, or just wander across the camp into the woods at dusk, stirring up animals as we went.

Kelsey, of course, would accompany me on these adventures. She was a bit afraid of the horses, having been stepped on by one once while I was putting on the saddle. After that, she would never come very close to the corral, and kept a safe distance as I rode, though would run alongside as we galloped. My brother's dogs went with him as well. He had a female German Shepherd and some type of Lab/Mastiff mix who weighed in at a whopping 130 pounds at that time.

Besides the rides, the horses provided other sources of amusement. It would not be uncommon to be watching TV late in the evening and see a horse's dark silhouette wander by the living room window of the house where my brother lived. Some would sneak by in their attempt at a great escape from the camp, whilst others were bolder, grabbing a quick glance through the picture window before they were out and about their business. On some mornings, you could see the noseprints left on the windowpane from the night before, not that we used those as evidence in some sort of *CSI* way, determining who

got free. We did not need to, the horses all moved in unison. If one got out, the other 39 played follow-the-leader!

As you might have guessed, any stray horse sightings were an indication that something was wrong, leading to immediate action on our part. The horses were behind a barbed wire fence in a field on the other end of the site. The director's house was the nearest thing to the old dirt road that led to nearby farms. If the horses got out, there was always some chance of danger. A horse could wander off down the road and into a car, onto an annoyed farmer's property, meet up with coyote, or get lost in the woods.

While the occasional funny TV-time horse sightings would occur, the majority of these happened in the middle of the night, on rainy evenings, or in the dead of winter when you had just settled in. The first alert was usually the dogs barking. We would get up to see a stray horse wandering by the house, then jump in the old, worn-down pickup truck. Sometimes, the dogs would leap into the bed of the truck; other times, they would run alongside, like some wild posse ready to do their duty in gathering up the runaways. We went off-road, feeling the bumps, headlights on high beam, probably driving too fast, and enjoying the connection of being brothers: one of us driving while the other was on the lookout for the herd. It usually didn't take long to find the horses.

Then the real chase began. We would try to outflank them and turn them back toward their field. It usually took finding the lead horse to get them back in line, though there were sometimes independent souls who made a break for it.

Everybody knew the drill: my brother, the dogs, the horses, and me. It was a part of an outdoor ballet conducted under the light of the moon; an occurrence so special that the initial annoyance of lost sleep, the cold at your back, or even wet feet was quickly forgotten. What we gained bordered on sacred. At first, my brother and I were representatives of the world of people, with Kelsey, my brother's dogs, and the horses part and parcel of the animal realm. But these differences quickly disappeared: all of us being both separate and together in those moments. We were a family of living creatures, and the rest did not matter.

After each outing my brother and I would feign annoyance while we discussed "those damn horses." The dogs usually went for a midnight swim in the pond to cool themselves after the chase, and the horses went back in their field to plot another daring escape.

Looking back now, I cannot say with any certainty that the horses were intentionally acting on my behalf, but what I do know is that they were not the only ones who broke loose, even if for a few precious moments: moments which are etched on my memory as a permanent reminder of wildness.

What *is* wildness?

It has to do with feeling alive and free, becoming more aligned with the primal force, and seeing that same ancient quality in our surroundings. In men's lives, it also has to do with cutting loose from the constraints of distorted versions of masculinity. Our canine companions act as guide for a direct connection with nature, with one another, and with a playful attitude. Within the magic circle of play, life is different. Our animal friends help us reclaim the missing parts of ourselves and the world, and act as a reminder of a long ago time when we walked side-by-side, making tracks in unknown territories. Those tracks are unencumbered by the wearing of shoes or boots and look remarkably similar: like two wild animals on the move.

5

Attachment and loss – two sides of the same coin

"Probably in all normal people, attachment continues in one form or another throughout life ..."
– Psychoanalyst John Bowlby

"The moment when someone can participate in another's lived story ... a different kind of human contact is created."
– Psychoanalyst Daniel Stern

One cold Kansas morning, I found myself swimming around in icy waters, and some might be tempted to believe that I was part of a 'polar bear club,' completing an annual New Year's Day swim. Instead, I was retrieving Kelsey.

We resided most of the year further south in Texas and as a puppy, Kelsey had not seen snow and ice before. During a morning walk in the woods, a rabbit happened to cross our path, and Kelsey enthusiastically pursued this across a frozen pond, sliding on the surface until she broke through the ice. I think back to that exact moment, almost twenty-five years ago, and how I, without hesitation, leapt in after her.

After that incident, Kelsey and I looked at each other in a different way. While we were already bonded, she seemed far more protective of my well-

being. One example of this was that, if someone stood over me as I sat in a chair, she would growl uncomfortably, baring her teeth. I learned later that height plays an important role in a dog's perspective of power and safety, and Kelsey was not okay with a potential imbalance that did not favor me, so meant to drive away the perceived foe, or at least bring them down to size.

I had my own transition where our bond deepened in a way I had not experienced before. She became my number one concern. I needed to know she was okay, sometimes to the annoyance of others. One time I was late for a friend's birthday party at a local restaurant, and happened to have Kelsey with me. I was not about to leave her in the car with the warm, afternoon Texas sun still high overhead, so I put her on the leash and headed for the front door. The plan was to poke my head in, hoping to see my friends. I would signal to them I was taking Kelsey home and then return shortly. As I pulled open the door, I literally walked right into the hostess. She met me with a sneer that did not seem entirely related to bumping into her. I was expecting some reaction about dogs, restaurants, and health regulations. Then she paused, did a double-take, looked at me in my sunglasses, down at Kelsey on the lead, and then surprisingly softened. My thought was, "Okay, maybe she *is* a dog person." I asked about my friends, and she began enquiring what they looked like, then trailed off awkwardly mid-sentence. At this point I realized she thought I was visually impaired, and Kelsey was my guide dog. I am not proud of what happened next. Not my finest moment. In vague terms I described my buddy to her, and she then led us to the table, where I offered birthday wishes for a few awkward moments with Kelsey at my side.

All noteworthy relationships have their turning points, places where we either double-down or fold. The events that transpired at the pond were, for me, even more significant. They were, in essence, an initiation rite. Before jumping into that icy water, Kelsey and I were a connected dog and owner, but upon our return we were on track to becoming companions. The trajectory of our bond would now move in a new direction; one that would shape my life. The watery encounter was also a two-sided experience. On one hand, it deepened my tie to Kelsey, and on the other, it made me aware for the first time that one day we would be parted. I tucked that last part into the deeper corners of my mind, stored beside other encounters and stories of loss from when I was growing up.

An occurrence near a creek

I never met Uncle Herman, though felt that I knew him through the recollections my mother shared when I was a boy. I assumed that Herman was a young man when he died, only to later learn that he was not much older than a toddler. He continued to age in my mother's mind, his story continually being revised and updated as she acquired new bits and pieces of our family mythology concerning his death. It would seem natural for any sister to have this type of preoccupation about a brother who met an untimely end. She would even say that she loved and missed him, which I assumed meant that they had an established relationship. I only found out much later that my mother was just a newborn when he passed.

The story I patched together was that, shortly after giving birth to my mother, my grandmother lost her oldest child, Herman, to an unexpected illness. Mortality rates were still high back in the 1920s, and there existed a number of illnesses that we do not hear mentioned much today. Before the widespread availability of antibiotics, Scarlet Fever was a major cause of childhood death, and, in my uncle's case, help came too late. Grief-stricken, my grandmother wandered into the woods, laid her newborn daughter near a creek, and walked away.

Some versions of this story have a fairytale-like quality. In one, the baby was placed on the rocks in a rapidly moving body of water, surrounded by water moccasins ready to strike at any second. By chance, a kindly neighbor from another farm found and rescued the baby; or maybe it was my grandfather, who becomes a pillar of safety in many other stories. When noting his daughter's absence in the house, he searches the woods, fords a stream, and brings her safely home. Thereafter, he keeps a special watchful eye on her, instilling a felt sense of security amid the retelling of a frightening story that would later be talked *about* at a number of family gatherings, but never really talked *through*. Whatever the actual events, themes of loss were set in place as a foundation for subsequent losses.

I have vivid recollections of going to a number of funerals as a boy. Within a few short years, my mother lost more than her fair share of relatives, including her father, mother, sisters, nephews, and, much later, one of her adult children. As a young boy, I remember our old rotary dial telephone ringing. My mother would always answer it in a welcoming southern accent. However, on certain occasions there was a long, drawn-out silence after that initial 'Hello:' someone on the other end was offering an explanation of what happened this time, and who it was that had passed away. The next sound that occurred was my mother placing the receiver back in the phone cradle, and then bursting into tears. Most of these were unexpected moments of loss signaled by a bell residing within a black steel and plastic machine: a ring that sometimes became a harbinger of death. Even as a bystander, trying to take these things in as a child, they felt sharp and beyond what I could absorb. My mother seemed to disintegrate before my eyes. The losses also seemed like something more than she could bear. There were other versions of loss to which I was sometimes more than a witness. The build-up to these was slower, but nonetheless still apparently unstoppable.

I previously mentioned having had a gentle German Shepherd when I was growing up, named Scooby after a cartoon character in a program I greatly enjoyed watching. Besides being a confidant who specialized in excellent listening skills for my own moments of vulnerability, he also loved to play, and would wear out your arm from throwing a tennis ball in his eagerness to retrieve it.

As he began to age, my mother would make strange comments about what to do with him now as he slowed down. These remarks made me anxious, and I tried to put them out of my mind. I was sure nothing would happen to our friend. One day, I came home from school and called for him. I looked in all the places he might be. While still searching, my mother came into the backyard to inform me that she had sent him to be with other gentle German Shepherds, where he could happily live out his remaining years chasing tennis balls and playing with his own kind. She tried to convince me that this was a good thing for everyone involved, but I just walked away without saying a word, sat in our shed with the door pulled shut, and cried.

Even as a child, I realized that when she was in a panicked frame of mind, there was no negotiating, no turning back from the decision. It was final. My mother would take some immediate action to ward off the threat, with seemingly little consideration for the long-term consequences, even if they would eventually have negative repercussions for her or those around her.

Many years later, a related scenario occurred, this time with my mom's own dog, another German Shepherd who she truly loved. When visiting from graduate school one time, I asked where her dog, Babe, was. She relayed the story with no filters or defenses, just raw regret. It was a more honest account than any other discussion involving human relations I ever heard her share. Babe was in the backyard having a senior moment, seeming a bit confused, getting tangled in some laundry hanging from a clothesline. It was too much for my mother, thinking that his behavior was a sign he would die soon. While weeping, she told me that she called the Humane Society. Babe seemed even more confused when strangers loaded him into a truck, she said. She kept a safe distance, viewing the entire scene from her window.

My mother was deeply afraid of loss, which also had implications for how she attached. She was often anxious and preoccupied with her children and her husbands. Back before there were cell phones and unlimited long-distance plans, she would rack up huge phone bills trying to keep tabs on everyone. Even when I left home for college and later graduate school, she would say, "I will worry about you till you get back. Call me so I can stop worrying." I am not sure if the worry was a magical way to keep me safe, or if it acted as a way to ward off her own fears of loss, or both. What I do know is her genuine warmth and care could be overshadowed by a frantic and sometimes demanding way of relating. When any hints of imaginable loss were in the air, she would mobilize her forces to neutralize these threats as quickly as possible. That need to escape through any means necessary was apparent to those she had relationships with, and to those who would have befriended her. This level of anxiety also impacted how she dealt with aging dogs. Though she clearly loved them, they were subjected to the same fear-based decisions that were later deeply regretted. Her dread of death unwittingly did the thing she was most afraid of – drove others away.

Some might be tempted to trace the beginnings of my mother's fear of loss to that occurrence by the creek. I think that was a defining event my mother puzzled over most of her life. While she had no actual memory of it, it was relived in various ways with her own mother, including stories that were told at holiday gatherings, and interactions that followed where I would see my mother – a grown woman with eight children of her own – suddenly turn into a shy, deferring girl, as though something big was still at stake: a 'something' that points to a deeply held insecurity of being left alone again, utterly vulnerable, without access to the comfort of others.

My mom left behind a legacy of anxieties associated with attachment and loss. On the surface, my solution was different. In many of my human relations I leaned away – a more avoidant style of attaching – which included shying away from people who were too eager to be in my space. I did not trust their readiness to engage. It seemed suspicious, maybe even potentially dangerous or exploitative; at least this is what I told myself when using this defensive strategy. Even with those that I wanted a closer tie to, there was a struggle. This was new terrain that I did not always know how to negotiate, and if things got too bumpy, I told myself this was something that I did not need. Of course, this aligned with what I learned about being a man: self-sufficiency is a mark of masculinity. My way of dealing with the fruits that fell from my family tree were temporary measures that ultimately left me unprepared when real loss eventually happened.

The only exception to my typical rules of disengagement was how I interacted with my animal friends. We found an easy way of being together that was not overwhelming, and did not seem to counter the rules of masculinity. I often thought about why it seemed so easy with them, but so much harder with people. Animals had not raised me, but there were moments when I felt like they were more like me than my own kin. I searched for and found explanations about why on both sides of the coin involving attachment and loss.

Attachment and loss

It may seem out of place in a discussion about grief to continue talking about attachment. Upon closer examination, though, my experiences suggest that attachment and loss are actually two sides of the same coin. Attachment-related issues, such as having our needs met and in what specific ways, set the stage for how the loss of a significant friend, family member, or animal companion is ultimately faced. Each of us has a unique background of experiences – some good and others bad – and each impacts how grief is approached, and the meanings attributed to loss. There can be various social, psychological, and physical factors to consider when understanding a person's own unique pattern of grieving: an approach as distinctive as a fingerprint.[1] It would not be entirely sufficient to reduce all of these complexities to one category, but much can be understood about our experience of loss by knowing about its counterpart in the shape of attachment figures.

Attachment figures

In its original usage, an attachment figure was defined as a caregiver with whom a child forms a deep and lasting emotional bond.[2] More specifically, a caregiver offers a special type of connection that is exceptionally important, involving qualities that seem irreplaceable. While a meaningful tie can be made with a number of friends, teachers, and family members, the place of an attachment figure is unique in a child's life.

Over time, the attachment figure label that was initially applied to the caregiver-child relationship has been expanded, and now also plays a role in adult romantic relationships, and even in the bond with animal companions. Across all these different scenarios, our attachment figures represent a lifeline providing a source of comfort when in distress, and one offering encouragement when facing difficult life challenges. Taking a few minutes to understand why this type of bond is so important sheds light on what is potentially lost when an attachment figure passes away.

The first element of what an attachment figure provides is referred to as a secure base, from which children can explore the world and take in new possibilities.[3] This aspect helps one's personality mature and take on new, previously unrealized dimensions. Without a secure base, children will not recognize their full potential. Growing up, a person who fills the attachment figure role is needed in order to explore the world on what feels like day trips across the mysterious realm of places like the kitchen floor. While it may seem like a few small squares of linoleum for us, it is actually one

giant leap for baby-kind. In order to accomplish the enormous feat of vast exploration, this 'special someone' provides a safe base from which the child moves back and forth, slowly taking in a new occurrence. Encouragement allows the child to engage with unfamiliar opportunities and people, from which they can pull back to safety, processing the experience, which eventually allows for further expansion. An attachment figure becomes a dependable resource; one that offers the get-up-and-go to eventually see the world beyond our own port of origin. The same concept is what helps children meet potential new friends on the playground, eventually be separated from their caregivers to go to school, or even one day leave the proverbial family nest entirely.

The secure base notion can certainly be applied to adult relationships, and relying on each other as a dependable source of support. Our big mission is more involved than successfully scampering across the floor, but the same spirit of backing is gained from our grown-up attachment figures.

For most, this is our best friend, romantic partner, significant other, husband, or wife. After a long day of work, most of us look forward to decompressing. Our bond also offers encouragement, setting the stage for tackling the world and its challenges again the following morning. It is through this connection that many of us adapt to difficult life circumstances, such as new jobs, or demanding bosses, and even in dealing with the remnants of childhood issues. Adults grow and develop more nuanced aspects of their identity with the right amount of reassurance to face difficult scenarios.

Likewise, an animal companion can assume the role of dependable ally, providing the psychological reassurance to take on challenging tasks. These might include taking hikes into a new area not previously explored, say, or it can be a more urban expansion where an animal friend doubles as a wingman, helping us find the courage to meet and greet new people at the local dog park. For some, it involves facing difficult life conditions, such as ending relationships, managing health issues, or even when a career path makes a sudden, unexpected stop. Animal companions help push us forward, encouraging bold steps we might not otherwise make. It is from within the safety of the bond that many develop further capacities, and discover new aspects of their personality.

Another facet of an attachment figure involves being a safe haven in times of distress.[4] John Bowlby talked about the important hardwired aspect as the human-animal to find safety when threatened or in danger. But instead of burrowing into a den, the preference is to nuzzle into the arms or care of an attachment figure. Needless to say, this quality is something everyone seeks with a caregiver as a child, and then later as adult, with a human significant other.

Our animal companions can also be a safe haven, providing predictable comfort in stressful times. They have the ability to sooth our worries and provide assurance that all will be okay. Given what was discussed in a previous chapter about their unique ability to accompany us in life's adventures, and even be attuned to our emotions based on our facial cues, it makes sense that dogs are experienced as the real shelter from the storm. There is something very calming about the tactile experience of our animal friends.[5] Research supports the idea that both our blood pressure and heartbeat begin to drop when petting and stroking their fur. There is also a relatively new line of study looking at how our companion animals influence us at the hormonal level. Research on oxytocin, what is sometimes referred to as the 'bonding hormone,' has shown that levels increase in a number of scenarios, such as when gazing at our dog.[6] In these moments, an animal companion becomes a safe haven.

Given the importance of these first two aspects of an attachment figure, it makes sense that there is a desire to be physically close to our attachment figures, something called 'proximity seeking.'[7] In their company, there is both security and joy. In Freud's later years, his Golden Chow, Jo-fe, was omnipresent in his consultation room as he saw patients, one of whom later remarked he was less concerned about Freud liking him than that his dog did. Jo-fe apparently had a way of screening would-be patients at the door.[8] After the initial meet-and-greet and approval, she settled into her own couch until the therapy hour concluded. It was rumored that the dog had an uncanny sense of time, and Freud had no need for a clock, as Jo-fe would rise from her spot when the session was over.

In modern times, our own version of proximity-seeking plays out in everyday events, including having animal companions accompany us on a drive to the grocery store, working through the chore list on a Saturday morning, and even when planning vacations at dog-friendly hotels. It should come as no surprise that recent research suggests that one in five dogs sleep in their human companions' beds.[9]

The flipside of the joy of being physically close is the pain of being apart. This fourth aspect of an attachment figure involves separation distress/anxiety,[10] which can manifest as feeling a little ache when parted by the normal, day-to-day comings and goings, and even more so when apart for longer.

While an attachment figure may be missed when absent, the normal routine tells us to rely on a reunion sooner or later. The exception to the rule is when temporary separations give way to permanent losses. When an attachment figure passes away or is lost, this understandably prompts feelings of grief. Something very real and substantial is subtracted from our lives: both the attachment figure and their safe, supportive ways of caring. As research suggests, the four attachment dimensions not only play a role in human companions, but also animal ones.

One recent study examined how the attachment figure's

characteristics, especially the safe haven quality, being a source of comfort when distressed, play a prominent role within the human-animal bond.[11] Devoted, middle-aged dog owners were asked to compare their animal companions to various human ones on attachment-related dimensions. The results found that approximatively 45 percent of dog people rated their canine companions higher on attachment features compared to that of their human family and friends.

There was also an important finding regarding middle-aged men and attachment. While males followed the general trend of the attachment figure findings, they were even more likely to rely on their dogs for emotional support when in distress than any other potential human supporters. The only tie that rivaled the bond between man and dog was their significant other. These findings support the notion that dogs really are 'man's best friend.' This adage may be especially true for men who feel alone and are not at ease revealing personal matters to others. Unfortunately, this state of being can be an all- too-familiar one for many men.

The attachment figure research also fits with two important points regarding men, one being that men are prone to find themselves in a social support bottleneck, sometimes reduced to just one person, and, with the exception of their romantic partners, men's one-to-one relationships tend to be less emotionally intimate.[12] Ultimately, men are not only faced with fewer chances to connect, but also frequently miss out on the opportunities that do exist.

These two relationship barriers are derived from male socialization, where males are discouraged from developing the skillset that enables deeper bonds. That is not to say that men cannot acquire the tools needed, it just may feel that doing so breaks the rules of manhood.

Oftentimes men attempt to meet a wide range of emotional needs from a single or very limited number of supports. While this occurrence can put undue pressure on those few resources that do exist, and place men in a vulnerable situation when they are lost, this approach fits with male socialization. It is more okay to have a confidant or sidekick, but not really an intimate tie with more than a few of those people who friended you on Facebook.

With all these challenges on the attachment front, the meaning of the bond with an animal companion can take on a unique dimension for men; one that is more all-encompassing in our relational world. The time spent with an animal companion is a deep connection that is also a respite from the world of being a man.

What makes this possible is the animal being a safe attachment figure; one who does not mind our shortcomings, or, at least, is not as willing to talk about them. For many men, dogs become a central player in our everyday existence, which is all the more reason to understand what is at stake for human companions when losing this vital connection.

Topsy

In 1937, psychoanalyst Marie Bonaparte, the granddaughter of Emperor Napoleon Bonaparte, published her book, *Topsy: The Story of a Golden-haired Chow.*[13] By today's standards, *Topsy* fits within the memoir literary genre: a personal account of how an animal companion has a deep and lasting impact on one's life. In the book, Bonaparte takes the reader through a series of journal-like entries, revealing both the intimate and sometimes raw exploration of her thoughts, feelings, and reactions, all of which are connected to Topsy, her "golden-haired Chow."

Ironically, the story begins with Bonaparte confessing her initial stance of emotional distance from Topsy, at times spending weeks and even months away from her while traveling out of the country. Only after being told her dog has a cancerous tumor on the lip does Bonaparte begin to embrace the attachment that has formed. In fact, Topsy's illness is the turning point for what may seem like indifference to a complex set of emotional responses especially important in the context of attachment and loss.

Bonaparte's relationship with Topsy also supplies the motivation for uncovering her own personal concerns, like fear of aging and dying. The book's journaling style pulls back the deepest private layers from her past, revealing themes of loss. Topsy's illness reminded Bonaparte of her father's unsuccessful and difficult bout with cancer. It also helps provide the reason why she has been against having another dog in the house for many years, even at her family's urging: dogs also pass away. As a girl, Bonaparte had many animals in her life, including a Fox Terrier named Satellite, whose death, Bonaparte discloses, "dimmed the sun's brightness and flowers for days."

Bonaparte moves further inward, also recalling the stories she was told concerning her mother's death as the result of a complicated pregnancy and difficulties during childbirth. She also has poignant memories of the beloved nurse "standing guard" at the bedside, assuring her as a child "that death would not enter" to take the young princess as well.

Attachment and loss are themes that shaped Bonaparte's life. Her wish as an adult had been to keep a safe distance from anything too temporary, signifying how fragile life could be. One solution was not to allow any more animal companions in the house, though she finally relents when her own young daughter falls ill and makes an impassioned plea.

But now the years have passed. Bonaparte is older, her children have grown and moved away, and she feels increasingly defenseless against what seems to be a series of losses that lay claim to her attention. Bonaparte is confronted with various forms of anxiety and unresolved grief, all of which seem to be evoked by her relationship with Topsy.

The book ends on a more even note. Topsy recovers, and perhaps Bonaparte does as well. The psychological space created during Topsy's illness has begun

much-needed grief work affecting both attachment and loss. A re-sorting is accomplished by visiting matters from the past, as well as issues that currently lay claim to her attention. Through the twists and turns of the journey she gains a new perspective on her relationship with Topsy, as well as past events from her own life. Without this important work, Bonaparte might have missed the opportunity to sort through the many faces of her grief.

I read Bonaparte's book about a year after Kelsey passed away. I found in her writings an imagined friend and colleague that also seemed to wrestle with some of the elements of avoidant attachment style, while caring deeply for her animal companion. I drew inspiration and encouragement from her honesty, and it helped me realize that, if I were to tell Kelsey's and Sadie's stories, I needed to do the same.

Psychoanalyst John Bowlby suggested that important losses in adulthood are particularly challenging when the current lost loved one is reminiscent of a caregiver from the formative years; one who performed essential psychological roles.[14] Maybe the role was as an emotional support that the cared-for person turned to when times were tough. Equally important is when the lost one was unique in their own right, adding something to our lives that was missing as we grew up. Once gone, there is the fear that those special qualities are lost forever and will never be experienced again. I knew Kelsey supplied a feeling of belonging that I had been looking for all my life. Explaining it in more detail at the time after she passed was a daunting task. I just felt empty and set adrift. My world felt poorer for Kelsey's loss.

The loss of an animal companion can open the way for other important grief reactions to be explored, ones that may not yet be fully addressed. Being such a catalyst attests to an animal companion's standing in our lives, showing the special place they occupy. Grief is the other side of attachment found in our own real-life stories, as well as memoirs, such as those written by Marie Bonaparte about her dog, Topsy.

Roles in our lives

Another important aspect of Bonaparte's approach to which I related was how Topsy played many roles over the course of their time together, which seemed to morph in response to other life events that were occurring. Topsy was sometimes her child substitute, for example; at other times her confidant, family member, protector, and friend. Bonaparte's relationship with Topsy was multi-faceted. At heart, Topsy was a source of emotional and psychological support, fulfilling one of the quintessential characteristics of an attachment figure: feeling irreplaceable.

One of the many ways to consider the impact of an animal companion on one's life is that he or she essentially assumes a psychological job on our behalf. While there is no formal notification from the Human Resources department about their exact duties, or length of contract,

in most cases the nature of the relationship takes its own unique course. What complicates matters is that, like any entry-level position, there is the possibility for duties to evolve over time.

For instance, it might be expected that a puppy's first job of looking cute and being cuddly changes. This might include being transferred to the security department; protecting the home from intruders. It could involve a promotion to human support services, where there is an opportunity for people to rely on an animal companion for emotional reassurance. Or perhaps our dog juggles these and other tasks all at once, multi-tasking on our behalf.

Recently, psychologist Dr Sue Ellen Brown investigated the role that animal companions play in fulfilling various psychological jobs to help maintain our sense of well-being.[15] In more technical psychological terms, these special types of helper are sometimes referred to as 'self-objects,' because they perform duties that aid and bolster the emotional health and well-being of our identities. The duties can include soothing us during moments of distress, taking on the role of challenging us to become better people, and, of course, through sheer single-minded devotion, acknowledging our lovability. While it may seem that the need for such a person or animal companion fulfilling these roles is primarily found in the formative years, even with a fully functioning adult there is an ongoing necessity for a trusted supporter, albeit in keeping with more mature expectations. People never outgrow the importance of self-objects. Dr Brown suggests that the presence of a supportive other may be especially important for those who have experienced attachment difficulties, loneliness, and trauma.

In one study Dr Brown found that 67 percent of respondents confirmed their animal companions performed at least two psychological roles, such as providing emotional nurturing and inspiring the growth of a better part of ourselves.[16] Through interaction with their animal companions, participants in the study felt like they were the most important person, and were provided with a sense of unconditional love and acceptance: qualities not easily supplied by any human companion. This kind of devotion led to a sense of being valued, special, and vibrant, as if the emotional sustenance received literally propelled one forward through life's journey. One participant stated that, in terms of her dog, "… that's her mission in life, and her job in life was to be with me."

Other types of roles included not only viewing an animal companion as a strong, protective, or wise friend, but also personally drawing from *their* qualities. Sometimes an animal companion had a trait or characteristic that the person lacked. Dr Brown noted that one of her participants, an elderly woman, felt empowered by being in the presence of her dog, who literally saved her life during a robbery. Likewise, being away from her animal companion left her with the sense of being diminished. In the case of this woman, she much admired her dog for knowing who could be trusted, a skill she did not possess. So, one of the roles that animal companions assume is as someone who has ideal qualities that we have yet to develop: a sort of lifecoach, providing encouragement to grow or do better.

The notion that animal companions assume such vital roles, even multitasking on our behalf, brings into focus our intense reactions to their loss. There are actually two losses: the animal themselves and the important function(s) they played in our life. Dr Brown mentions that the telltale sign of an animal companion who has been performing these essential psychological roles on our behalf is that the person receiving the support feels a strong emotional reaction when the connection is lost. It is more than just sadness; it is as though a part of us has gone missing, prompting a desperation to reunite, sadness, and emptiness.

Making these feelings even more complicated, the roles performed have both a significant impact, and change in step with life circumstances. So, to give a full account of the loss means to piece together the various places along the way that an animal companion lent support. Some of the specifics may have been temporarily forgotten over the years (telling the story in its entirety may allow recovery of these) but doing so allows the meaning and significance of the bond to become even clearer.

I know I felt encouraged and understood when reading

Bonaparte's book about Topsy. It also got me thinking about the various universal roles that animal companions play in our lives. Given the amount of complexity involved, there needs to be a way to summarize the deeper importance of the bond. Something I like to think of as 'the dog pack.'

The dog pack

I have been searching for the meaning of the bond, and, more specifically, my bond with Kelsey. This is more than just a hobby, a curiosity, or the desire to have the needed words when people ask me, "Why was she so important to you?" It felt like I could not complete that next step in our continuing bond without knowing 'Why?' Part of what perplexed me for so long was looking for one all-encompassing answer, while in reality there are many. There are many reasons why I needed, and still need, that connection with an animal companion.

In my mind's eye I picture a group of characteristics that enrich my life – a dog pack of sorts. When it is assembled, I feel more whole, like all the pieces of me are present. I am able to relate to myself, nature, and those I love differently. When the pack is absent, I search, hoping to find its members again, hidden behind a tree or over the next horizon. I have talked about these members before, but imagine bringing them all together. Each unique characteristic acts as a type of 'attachment cue,' prompting us to realize that an animal companion is a viable attachment figure.

These attachment cues tell us this connection is safe, and speaks to a deep need we all have to make and sustain a meaningful bond throughout our lives.

The first member of my dog pack is accompaniment. A canine companion provides a sense of connection, a constant presence through life's ups and downs. Given that humans are social creatures, hardwired to make and sustain a bond with at least one other, life becomes more meaningful when someone else is there to share the experience.

Another pack member is acceptance, a quality especially important in a world where many feel pressured to assume a permanent persona. Over time, and through the give and take that marks any real and lasting relationship, the stage for a pure love connection is set: love without ambivalence; a full range of deep feelings without fear. The love is distilled to its purest elements.

Our animal companions provide a sense of attunement, argued by many to be among the most quintessential of psychological needs. Dogs have a unique ability to track and respond to human facial expressions and shifts in our behaviors. They can provide 'alerting responses' to these changes in our emotional and physical well-being. That is, they scan the situation and respond in-kind to what is happening. This can involve discerning our good and bad moods, and even acknowledging when there is a physical change, such as noting the onset of a migraine. When canine companions react to what is going on in our lives through a happy tail wag, or a well-placed paw indicating support, all of these are acts of offering attunement. They create the psychological experience of having been heard; even understood. Feeling understood and cared for are key elements that help us decompress from the daily grind, when times turn tough, but also as a central part of celebrating life.

Animal companions assume an inspirational role in our lives. The encouraging aspect of the bond helps us develop capacities, skills, and previously unrealized dimensions of our personality. Sometimes our companions have ideal qualities that one wishes to cultivate, and other times our dogs provide situation-specific guidance for what we might aspire to become. This is a mix of life coach and moral guide.

In the presence of animal companions, there is an opportunity to reclaim a part of the primal past modernity has left behind, or a sense of wildness and a chance to feel alive, which includes the joy of play found at dog parks, in backyards, and on wooded hiking trails. Wildness is another way dogs invite us to become immersed in life.

In a recent study, we found that men really do consider their canine companions as potential multi-taskers across various dimensions in their lives. We developed a questionnaire – 'The Companion Animals Roles Scale (CARS)'[17] representing three general dimensions regarding men's connections with dogs: an Emotional Bond aspect, one related to Personal Growth, and Lifestyle Roles.

The Emotional Bond has to do with the deep connection men feel with their dogs, and consists of the following descriptors: Friend, Confidant, Emotional Support, Family Member, Helpful Throughout Life Tough Times, Share Good Times With, Unconditional Love, and Watch TV/Movies With. The Personal Growth factor involves changes and transformations men attribute to the bond with their dogs, and includes the following descriptors: Helps Meet and Socialize, Instills Hope, and Teacher of Life Lessons. Lastly, the Lifestyle aspects of men's relationships with their dogs represents day-to-day roles, including: Exercise Partner, Home Security Protector, Medical Assistance, and Playmate for Children.

The results from the CARS study also held special significance for males wrestling with one of the quintessential challenges of being a man in Western culture: labeling and understanding their own feelings and those of others. We have discussed this issue in a previous chapter as 'Normative male alexithymia.' These same men perceived their dogs to be promoting various facets of their personal growth, including expanding social networks, learning various life lessons, and helping sustain hope. All of these characteristics are of value in their own right, but perhaps take on unique meaning in the lives of many men who struggle with conflictng aspects of male socialization.

The dog pack is more than the sum of its parts. The bond is a unique relationship offering the chance to relax the stringent roles of being man. Our connection with animal companions becomes a safe refuge. For some males a positive, secure connection with an animal companion counterbalances a history of insecure types of attachment with human companions, family, friends, and significant others. This sets the stage for personal transformation, allowing men to rethink dysfunctional ways of being masculine, and grow in more relational ways with both human and animal companions. The bond can prompt a search for deep personal meaning, or help turn attention to matters of transcendence/spirituality. Our canine companions assist us in learning more about the perspectives of others and responding in-step to their needs. In short, dogs help their male companions become better, healthier men.

Bringing the dog pack together ushers us into a new state of relationship readiness, or at least allows for one meaningful tie in the context of a relational world that can feel daunting and confusing. Our dogs are one-part friend and another part life coach. When the elements of the dog pack take hold in a person's life, this has an impact. For many of us, the experience counters the everyday crisis of connection with ourselves and the world around us. A canine companion helps breathe new life into weary souls. The first occurrence of these experiences draws one to the threshold of forming a new friendship, but when it has occurred innumerable times over the course of ten to fourteen years, a 'pet' morphs into what can best be described as an animal companion. It is little wonder that research on the human-animal bond reveals that upwards of 85 percent of people describe their animal companions as like a family member or close friend.[18] On the other side, of course, is a similar level of intensity when an animal companion is lost; having its own unique meaning in men's lives.

Research also suggests that the number of single adults with animal companions is on the rise, increasing over 16 percent (from 2006 to 2011).[19] This includes a 27.7 percent increase in animal companion ownership among males living alone, and at the time I lost Kelsey, I was one of them.

This leads us back to the main point of this chapter concerning the interrelated experience of attachment and loss – the depth of attachment is mirrored by the intensity of loss … a topic I know something about myself.

Doggy doors are magical portals

I was in the process of many life transitions, including changing jobs and moving out of state, and was gone for the better part of two weeks. Before the trip, Kelsey seemed to be having some trouble with her peripheral vision. If a hand passed too quickly from the side of her head to the front, she appeared startled, as if the hand had magically appeared out of thin air. I looked into her green eyes, which now seemed a little cloudy, and wondered if cataracts were setting in. I told myself I would deal with this straight away when I came home. In retrospect, this was something I did not really want to acknowledge as a 'real problem,' hoping it would clear up on its own, like some fluke. Looking back, my discomfort centered upon admitting that Kelsey was getting old.

Kelsey had always been such a healthy dog. We had only been to the vet for some type of sickness a few times in nearly 14 years. I suppose some part of me wondered if her apparent invincibility meant she would always be around. I think I took that for granted. When I came home from my business trip, I noticed Kelsey heading for a piece of furniture in the house, and then, at the last moment, stumbling and barely missing a head-on collision. This happened more than once. She also did not seem herself in other ways. Perhaps most disturbing was that Kelsey, formerly the master of negotiating all doggy doors both big and small, now seemed hesitant when approaching it.

There had always been a doggy door for Kelsey in the houses I owned, and most of those I rented. Sometimes I had to be creative, like turning a glass sliding door into a partial dog door, or cutting a panel into an existing wooden door, or even once, when there was no possibility of a doggy door proper, using a very low-laying window.

I remember a conversation I had when remodeling the old 1930s Houston Tudor brick house we lived in. The contractor thought that a misplaced dog door which allowed entry to the living room would not only significantly impact the house's aesthetic charm, but also its potential resale value. In my mind, there was no other place to put it, and going without one was not an option. So, in my newly remodeled living room were beautifully refinished hardwoods, mortise tendon mission-style furniture that I painstakingly hand-built, a collection of antique stained glass I had collected over the years, some original art ... and a big, white plastic dog door leading to the backyard.

The last place I lived without a dog door was a small basement apartment I rented when on internship. Even in her prime, Kelsey could not make it eight hours without going out, and I didn't want to subject her to that sort of trouble anyway. I learned quickly the first week of internship that if I did not make it home for lunch my bag would be covered with the nervous remains of Kelsey's breakfast. So, almost every lunch hour of that year-long internship, I would schedule my day around leaving a few minutes early to walk up the hill to my car, race home for 15 minutes, grab Kelsey's lead and walk her as quickly as I could around the block, hoping she would 'do her business.' I would then sprint back, eating as I drove, and rush back to the center where I worked, usually with indigestion. I felt like I was constantly late, always coming back to work sweating and burping.

For me, the availability of doggy doors was a sign that I was taking care of Kelsey. Not only could she come and go outside as she pleased to relieve herself, she could also watch squirrels, roll in the dirt, feel the sun on her fur, and generally do what dogs do. Doggy doors also have symbolic meaning, a magical portal of sorts. Kelsey was used to the passageway, and it helped her straddle the two worlds of the civilized and the wild. Her great-ancestors from that long ago time were accustomed to roaming freely here and there across the wilderness. I imagined that having a doggy door allowed Kelsey some illusionary contact with them by wandering to and fro into the backyard. Sadly, this gateway to the untamed world was now slowly closing. Kelsey was having trouble negotiating the ultimate representation of freedom for a domesticated canine.

The night before we went to the vet, her situation worsened. She was a little confused before, but now her mood was fearful. It seemed that the small window of sight remaining had begun to close. The look of fright in her eyes was hard to bear. Kelsey sat in my bedroom, urinating on the floor in the middle of the night. She shook. She got up and lost her bearings, bumping into things she had avoided a hundred times before. She didn't seem to know if it was night or day, or if she was in the backyard or in my room. When she was not asleep, she would stare into the distance. How can a doggy brain make sense of such a thing, the world slowly and permanently going dark?

I woke up every hour or so that night, fearing the worst.

We went to the vet the next morning. I had discovered years before that, in tense moments, Kelsey could somehow sense my level of ease or apprehension, responding in kind. I realized that I had to keep my own nerves in check, and then she could more or less lay on the floor until we were called. The difference this time was that, while I attempted to remain perfectly still, I could not stop the warm tears slowly rolling down my face. I am not a frequent crier as a general rule, though I do not begrudge tears or those who shed them. As I would learn over the next six months, sometimes they are the most appropriate response to the circumstances that surround us.

The vet came in to see Kelsey as if this were any run-of-the-mill visit. She asked what brought us in. I could not find the words. My face was squashed up. I would maybe say a word or two, before I clinched my teeth, trying not to let all the worry and anticipatory grief out: "I am sorry … she lost her sight … since I got home from my trip." The vet handled Kelsey gently, with real care. I am most grateful for that kindness. She did a complete work up, but the results were 'inconclusive.' It could be any number of things but was probably a degenerative condition, and we were referred to an eye specialist in Houston.

I loaded Kelsey in the passenger seat of the truck. All I had been trying to hold in came rolling out. My chest shook, and my eyes blurred. I put my hands on Kelsey and felt the softness of her fur: "I love you, old girl." This would become my catchphrase over the next few months to express all that I simultaneously felt. Sometimes there are no other words. I drove home that morning, realizing that my old friend was not invincible. We had stumbled, unexpectedly, onto the road that led to the end of our time together.

We all seek refuge from the storm

After making the long drive up from Texas, Kelsey did not like being inside our new house in Nashville. She was unsettled, nervous, and would go from lying perfectly still to making a dash for the door. The thing was, she did not know where it was, and nor did she have a map of it in her brain. This new place was strange to her. Making matters worse, she had lost nearly all of her sight. Kelsey would look for her familiar path of escape in our old home in Houston, only to stumble around, bumping into things that were out of place. She then became more panicked, which would often result in her old nervous response of relieving herself on the floor. So, when she was in the house, I would follow her around. Even if I thought she was settled, I would continue listening for her movements. The small sounds of restlessness stirring would eventually gather again, signaling the need for another trip to the backyard.

While Kelsey had always held dual citizenship, indoors and outdoors, her preference was clearly the backyard now. Except for the privacy fence that bordered the perimeter and the raised deck, it was an open and unrestricted area she seemed to enjoy lying under. She only occasionally bumped into something when finding the way to her new place of safety. By contrast, the layout of an old 1920s bungalow is cozy by design. This house was a never-ending gauntlet of unseen obstacles to negotiate; ones that seemed to unnerve her.

While Kelsey spent most of her time outdoors now, I initially insisted that she come inside when the weather was bad, even if it was just for a little while. Sometimes I would guide her from the backyard by her collar to encourage her to walk. As time went by, the rain fell harder, and she moved even slower, so I decided it was best just to pick her up and carry her inside. Kelsey would sit on the floor and I would towel her off. When it was cool outside, I would leave a warm blanket on top of her. She would sleep for maybe half-an-hour in the cozy bundle I made for her, and then be ready to go back outside – storm or not. I reluctantly guided her back outside, hoping it would be a quick visit, but oftentimes she hunkered down on the rain-covered ground. All that toweling off was undone, and she would not get up, even at my urging.

I could let this be for a bit, and maybe even go inside for a few minutes, but eventually I would bring her in again for another round of rub down and warm up. This dance we did during dire weather as it became fall resulted in me, more than a few times, being up and down for most of the night. I found myself becoming a devoted subscriber to the Weather Channel and upcoming forecasts. This became a challenging process for me, and I am sure for Kelsey as well. I was looking as haggard as Kelsey, and took quick naps when I could just to keep up.

Now, as I look back, I think Kelsey was ready to let go. She was preparing to return to the elements. Her physical appearance began to change. It was not just that she was old, because anybody who saw her knew that. She began taking on a simultaneous manifestation of wildness and decay, as if she was slowly becoming a part of the wooded landscape. Her fur looked feral and untamed, even when I brushed it. Her nails seemed to grow longer than I ever remembered. If you looked at her too hastily or with one eye shut, she seemed to take on a mysterious and sometimes otherworldly quality. In her movement toward becoming one with nature, she spent nearly all of her time in the backyard.

I thought a lot about how to respect what I was quickly realizing were our last days together. Chief among these considerations was being there for her when she passed. I spent many long hours contemplating that commitment and trying to do what I could to honor it.

Since Kelsey would not really stay inside the house, even during bad weather, I tried to make her a 'home' in the backyard. I got her an igloo house, then a regular-shaped doghouse, and, finally, I attached a doggy door to the garage. She tried each of these homes on for size, mostly at my urging. I would try the sweet sale of "What a great house," "You will like it in here, Kelsey," and so on. It seemed like she was humoring me by going inside, even lying down for a moment or two. For that minute, I would have the illusionary sense that Kelsey was now securely in place, only to see her suddenly try to get up and out the next moment. She had a fearful look in her eyes. All of these new places seemed to frighten her. Truth be told, she may not have known where she was walking, or that she was even inside some type of shelter. It may have just seemed like some strange, foreign realm. I felt frustrated and would bite my lip at each vain attempt to make her secure in her new permanent outside surroundings. On one occasion, I felt my anger rise, muttering, "Come on, damn it! I just want you to be safe." I did not realize at the time that her safety meant my safety, and her comfort meant that I could relax for minutes in the illusory state of all being well.

If I could not get Kelsey to stay inside or embrace the doghouse lifestyle, then I would try to make her as comfortable as possible outside. This included trying to accept the situation for what it was. I developed an evening ritual of visiting with Kelsey before I went to bed. Oftentimes, I would also go outside to check on her in the middle of the night, bad weather or not. The ceremony began when I, using my most gentle voice, would go over to her and say "Hey, old girl, how about I join you for a while?" As I positioned myself next to her, she would, in her own way, nuzzle against my leg. Sometimes I could feel the knots of tension in her back and I'd rub them out. Other times, I would just stroke her fur. After a few minutes of this, she would heave a big sigh and relax.

I would then tell her stories, our stories, all of which began with, "Remember when …" we did this or that. We'd reminisce about walks in the woods, her dog friends up in Kansas, or, my favorite, the day we met. Nine times out of ten, this resulted in me choking up. She would sometimes turn her head suddenly and look at me as I talked. It seemed as if she was saying, "Why are you so sad? I am the one dying here." Or maybe she did not understand how I could so quickly go from a soothing voice to one that was so broken up.

Sometimes our evening ritual stirred up Kelsey a bit, and I would take advantage by trying to get her to eat something. She had stopped eating dry food entirely and, on most occasions, she wouldn't even eat the canned stuff. So, I would slowly feed her bites of lunchmeat. She would gingerly take it from my hand, like doing so constituted a great effort on her part. I remembered, in years gone by, how the smell and taste of processed ham would drive her wild. I would make a sandwich and always save some for her. Now, sadly, it barely got a response.

The goodnight ritual always ended the same way: me covering her up with a blanket and later with my old shirts and coats. I guess if I was not there beside her, I wanted some part of me present. I hoped that this helped her feel safe and looked after. Kelsey would often tolerate this in my presence, but by morning check-in, the makeshift bedding had been deserted. As the garments became soiled or wet from the morning dew, I would bring out the next batch. I left the other stuff scattered around the yard because I figured Kelsey might stumble onto it and find some comfort. Eventually, my backyard started looking like I was doing laundry out there – my old stuff scattered about. I am sure my neighbors did not appreciate the Hillbilly-noir theme I was creating. They must have wondered if a whiskey still would soon follow, becoming the central accent piece, and completing my backyard design.

Sometimes, at night, Kelsey would let me lead her over to the makeshift shanty I built from a section of eight-foot fence that basically hung over the raised back porch. Her wooden canopy would be easier to get under than the raised porch, and could also protect her from rain or wind. Not that I wouldn't be out there if bad weather came, but in my mind the blankets, old clothing, and the shanty were all a refuge from the storm. In one sense, it was about the one that could unexpectedly appear on the Doppler radar; in another, it was the storm I knew was coming. Provisions needed to be in place for both.

One thing was certain, though, each of these nighttime visits ended with a deeper realization of the impermanence of life. I knew Kelsey's time was coming to an end. On one level, it was a curious thing for me to watch someone I knew and loved move slowly toward passing. Kelsey was teaching me another lesson about life and that was about its counterpart, death.

Most of us don't like death as a general rule. It seems so permanent – so forever. And yet, my old friend was demonstrating to me the true nature of life. Loss was a part of living and a part of caring. There were moments when I felt very alive being so close to my friend who was fading. It was like we had a lifeline, tautly held between the two of us. In those moments, my life seemed to find more tenderness than I had ever known before. I felt like I was touching the best part of me, and somehow transcending into something bigger.

Long goodbyes

It was a warm day in early November when Kelsey passed. Mid-afternoon came, and Kelsey was trying to move out of the sun, using a hit-and-miss approach to locate a cooler place in the backyard. When I saw her searching, I guided her to a shaded patch. She settled as well as she could in her new spot on the grass, but did not seem quite right. There was a stagger as I tried to move her. I had never seen her having trouble walking before. A friend of mine was visiting, and I asked, "Where do you draw the line? When do you call it quits and let her go?" He tried to delicately answer the question by saying nothing. I had been searching for the answer now for several months. What I did not know at the time

was that sometimes, between true companions, permission has to be given. A nod that says, "You have done enough, it is your turn to rest." In my mind, Kelsey was holding on for me, and I had trouble allowing her to go.

The afternoon cooled, and it began to turn dark. I was heading out to grab something to eat, and had made it only halfway down the road before I experienced the feeling that I needed to return home. So I returned and found Kelsey in the backyard. It was not long before she had a seizure. This sent panic through my bones. I realized in that moment that it was time – time to let her be at peace. Months of agonizing about a decision evaporated. To hang around in a so-so condition was marginally okay, but to be in pain drew the line. I would not let her suffer.

I stroked her fur, and after a few minutes, she stopped shaking. Her tongue was hanging out, and she was unable to draw it back in for a few moments. "Hang on, Kelsey; I am going to help you now – help you find some rest," I told her. I ran into the house and found the yellow pages. My vet had an emergency number that forwarded me to the animal hospital down the road. It was just a few minutes away.

I carried Kelsey to the backseat of the SUV, reminding myself I needed to be calm for her. I drove with one hand on the wheel and the other behind me on her fur. I kept stroking her and began using the phrase that I would begin repeating in different derivations for the next hour or so, "... going to let you rest now, Kelsey ... going to let you rest."

I pulled into the clinic parking lot, not sure whether to leave her in the truck or bring her in right away. Kelsey looked peaceful now in the backseat, as though the seizure had zapped her energy and perhaps her fear as well. I went inside and walked to the front desk. The other dog owners in the waiting room seemed to pick up the scent of something wrong. I am not sure why I did this, perhaps out of courtesy to the young puppy I saw in someone's arms, whose time I hoped was not up, or perhaps because Kelsey's passing seemed so incredibly private, but I whispered to the receptionist that I was the one who called about putting down his dog. I half-pleaded, "Should I bring her in now? Could we do this quickly, please?" She assured me that it would be just a few minutes while they got a room ready, and that she would come out to the truck.

We brought Kelsey into the room, and quickly discovered that the examination table made her uncomfortable. We moved her to the floor instead, resting on my legs. I stroked her fur and continued my chant about the peace that would soon arrive. The young vet who was on call came in and asked how much Kelsey weighed so he could calibrate the shot he needed to administer. He returned and said,

"She won't feel a thing; I'm just going to give her a shot first to relax her, then another one to help her go to sleep." I tried to cradle her body without making her feel overwhelmed. He made the injections, and she relaxed. The vet listened for her heart and said, "She is almost gone now ... she doesn't feel anything, but I need to give her one more shot to help her finish." And he did.

In the seconds that followed I felt Kelsey's spirit leave her body. I felt it rise up and leave the room and this earthly plane. It was very tangible to me, as if I could feel her moving on to another place. Somehow, that gave me some peace. This moment of passing that I had dreaded for months had come and gone. I had often fantasized that I might literally fade to black. I asked if I could have a few moments alone with her. The vet told me to take as much time as I needed.

I said my goodbyes to my friend. I tried to force into my mind how her fur felt, like touching it one more time after nearly fourteen years would somehow really drive it home in a way that I could not forget. I kissed her nose. I thanked her for all that she had done and been for me. 'Thank you' seemed jam-packed with more memories and gratitude than two words could contain. I said, "You rest now, girl." I looked into her eyes and knew that Kelsey had left the building.

6

Grief in the masculine world

"There is no despair so absolute as that which comes with our first great sorrow. Before we know what it is to have loved and lost, to despair and have recovered hope."
– George Eliot

"Only people who are capable of loving strongly can also suffer great sorrow, but this same necessity of loving serves to counteract their grief and heals them."
– Leo Tolstoy

Goodbyes

I never got a chance to say goodbye to my father, partly because he passed away suddenly, and also because our relationship had become strained over the preceding ten years.

When I moved from Texas to Nashville I thought I would see more of him since he lived only four hours away. We established the habit of meeting halfway for lunch on the weekends, and I even had him down for Thanksgiving once. Each time we met began the same way: he would share his long list of grievances against almost everyone he knew, and many others he did not. Even in restaurants, this was done with such intensity that the waitress would sometimes come over to ask if everything was all right. Once, I had seen my father reduce a poor, unsuspecting

car rental agent to tears. After the unsuccessful transaction, I asked if he was okay, and also if he registered the effect he had had on the crying young woman. His response was consistent with many previous ones: difficulty understanding his impact on other people. At some point in his later years, one of my siblings relayed to me that my father had 'officially given up' on me. I was never clear what the exact events were that warranted such a decision, but I do know that we had a long and complicated history.

My father told me he basically grew up without a father. My grandfather had emigrated from Yugoslavia as a boy, and worked in the steel mill in Pennsylvania all his life. When he was not down in the blast furnace on the job, he apparently was trying to avoid the furnace at home, where he and his wife fought, which meant long hours away and not much father- and son-time. My father said he and I spent more time together in a year than he and his father had in his lifetime. He saw our visits as a victory of sorts – that he was a better father than his own – but what he never seemed to account for was the quality of those interactions. He felt slighted easily, and could become full of rage.

As a little boy, I remember him fighting with my teenage half-brother, with me standing in-between, unsuccessfully trying to push them apart. I recall the unease I felt when he came home from work; how he would snap his leather belt and hang it on the doorknob, the jingle from the buckle announcing that the Lord of the Manor had arrived. For me, the worst was hearing how, in one of his fits of anger, he kicked his dog. I was never sure what prompted that, but the poor dog died a few days later.

Though I loved my father very much, and spent years working on our relationship, especially in my twenties and thirties, it was not his rage that would eventually make me take up a safe-distance position with him: it was disappointment and the accruing grief. I think our connection died of a broken heart. I look back now and realize we both held expectations of each other; some of which were talked about but obviously not worked through.

Adjusting expectations is a part of any long-term connection, especially concerning family. It involves revisiting old hopes and wishes from childhood, and trying very hard to work through

them. Some can include rigid and unrealistic childlike perspectives of perfection, ones that demand a caregiver to make up for what happened before there is any hope of reconciliation. Others can be punishing: 'I will hurt you by being distant, so you can know how it feels.' It is better if a more adult- like perspective can be eventually reached, where a parent is seen as a person in their own right, separate from their role as a would- be caregiver.

In order to accomplish a new, adult-to-adult relationship, sometimes losses and old hurts have to be mourned, with the recognition that they will never be made up for in the context of the parent-child dyad. There is a hope, however, that maybe more fulfilling connections will come along which speak to some of the deeper human needs, filtered through more grown up channels and expectations. A person can be loved as an adult – and the love may find its way into the raw parts that still hurt – but none of us get to be a child again. At least not in the ways we fantasize about, with regard to new and improved parents who suddenly appear on the scene, and make up for all that went before. I am sorry; that will not occur.

Over the last ten years of my father's life, I would scale back my hopes with each encounter. One day, I found myself on a shrinking iceberg; one barely big enough to stand on without falling into the water. With so much history beforehand, balancing on that small, slippery piece of ice left me feeling paralyzed. If I moved too much, there was a real risk of losing what remained. Yes, I wanted to see him, even after he boycotted my mother's funeral, or cited financial strain as the reason for not attending my wedding. He seemed to continually forget I was having trouble driving across town, much less long distances for lunch, due to medical issues that stretched on for years. He was older, now, and having memory troubles ... wasn't he? Or was this another way in which I was feeling frozen in place, trying to hang onto something? In either case, I wish I had been in a different place that afforded more room for dealing with these difficult issues at the time.

I also wish things had ended on a different note for my dad. He was pretty sad most of his life; maybe more so in the last years. I try to keep that in mind, and the good times we had along the way. When I was in my twenties, I found an old reel-to-reel tape recording of when I was an infant, no older than my son is now, on which I was surprised to hear my dad use a voice I had never heard him use before. He sounded happy and relaxed while he was playing with my brother and me, and it was not the burdened, angry tone to which I had grown accustomed. I have been thinking a lot about that memory recently.

There are some questions to consider regarding men's response to grief and loss. The range of potential losses can involve actual deaths of friends and family, but there are also symbolic ones to consider, like what it means to have unrealized dreams or conflicts that can be traced back to the formative years. While these things can clearly be rooted in our early history, they can also easily be found as a part of our everyday experience, unwittingly guiding aspects of our current relationships, or acting as the driving force behind one's work and striving for success.

Then there is the issue of matters such as getting older. Is a man still a man when past his physical prime, unable to do the things which marked his entrance to the masculine world, or not with the same level of intensity or skill, at least? Sometimes with aging it feels as though our bodies betray us. These various losses can press on our awareness, causing a re-sorting of life meanings and priorities.

In this chapter, the focus is how men are socialized to express grief, and the various personal meanings attributed to loss. Do men approach these important topics in a different way, and, if so, what does that look like? The answers ultimately give a nuanced understanding of the importance of our connections with others, including our canine companions.

What grieving looks like

Grief experts Kenneth Doka and Terry Martin suggest that, while gender does not solely determine one's reaction to bereavement, it certainly can have an impact.[1] These researchers note that socialization as a man or woman can influence how one is taught to process loss. At one end of the continuum is the intuitive griever, sometimes referred to as a 'heart griever,' who works through loss by concentrating heavily on experiencing emotions and potentially sharing them with others. This type of grief is the most recognized notion of what bereavement looks like, though, by definition, is difficult for some men to enact.

The heart grieving approach contains elements that break the rules of traditional masculinity: namely, an outward display of tender feelings, while also involving others in one's most private world. From the perspective of how many boys are taught to be men, sharing the content of our inner lives opens the door for awkward exchanges, and even moments of embarrassment or shame. Men are not always sure how to be vulnerable, especially when it entails loss. Turning to others in what can be construed as the ultimate form of asking for help, or, in the extreme, being helpless, also counters total self-sufficient masculinity; it pulls for the reaction that one has failed as a man. These types of overly-cautious or even skewed versions of support-seeking complicate the grieving process in ways some men are not prepared for. Sometimes it is easier to try another way instead.

At the other end of the continuum is the instrumental griever, also called the 'head griever.' The instrumental approach advocates 'mastery' over 'oneself,' the 'environment,' and 'one's feelings.' Here, the accent is on dealing with loss in a more private, introspective fashion, channeling reactions into mental or physical activity.

For instance, a head griever may retreat to the wood shop, work out at the gym, or even take action in support of some type of related cause after loss has occurred. Action is a way to burn off the intensity of emotions. It gives a focus, a way to turn something that feels intangible into a thing that can be physically touched. When one has finished the task for the day, it feels like progress is being made. Doka and Martin have found in their research that many men are socialized to approach grief in this more action-oriented, reserved, and reflective fashion.

Doka and Martin also note that many of us (both men and women) do not necessarily fit into either category of griever, but instead can ultimately adapt a blended style of heart and head grieving. Instead of occupying one end of the continuum or the other, a mixed approach does allow a wider range of skills to be utilized when dealing with loss. There may be times when self-reflection is utilized, and other times when one draws on the benefits of sharing with others. We can dial into intense feelings that then act as a guide for more action-oriented grief.

That said, learning to assume a blended style of grieving out of sheer necessity can be uncomfortable in the middle of a crisis. Building a new skillset when we are at our most vulnerable can be overwhelming, and men wanting to incorporate features of heart grieving, but who feel at odds about doing so due to the code of traditional masculinity, just adds to the dilemma. Doka and

Martin coined the phrase 'dissonant grievers' to represent those who experience grief naturally in one way (either heart or head style), but who are blocked from expressing or adapting to it.

For example, a man might experience the emotional aspect of grief, but feel guarded about expressing it openly because he perceives it as 'unmanly' to let others see him cry. Men learn to intentionally suppress feelings of sadness and loss, waiting for the right times to bring them back up, and this is sometimes referred to as 'sampling' grief or 'dosing.' On one hand, the approach makes grief work seem more manageable – picking it up when ready and then setting it down when not. On the other, grief can be stretched out over time, and sometimes there are missed spontaneous opportunities to work through loss when it arises. Given that male socialization plays a role in dosing, anger is another way around the dilemma of male socialization and mourning.

Men and anger

Anger plays a special role in the world of men. It is clearly an emotion which, when appearing alongside loss, would seemingly fall under the heart style of grieving. However, I would argue that it does not count per se as such in the traditional masculine experience. Men are taught to deal with loss by utilizing anger as a 'non-emotion.' Anger is a rare exception that does not break the stringent rules governing how to be a man, because it is perceived as both acceptable and manly.

Anger represents a masculine protest against uncontrollable circumstances: you are down, but certainly not out; still able to maintain a sense of dignity by registering an objection. In the case of grieving, anger can accomplish a similar purpose, protesting the loss in a socially sanctioned way that says the situation has not gotten the best of you.

Anger can also be an effective way to mask grief, especially for men. Grief is funneled along with other emotions that feel off-limits into one that is more acceptable. The problem with this approach is that not only can men deceive themselves into thinking nothing is wrong, but others are often misled as well. It may be difficult enough to be around the angry guy, even if you know he is grieving. What makes matters worse is when others do not know he has suffered a significant loss, or that this is his 'modus operandi' for expressing hurt. In reaction to an environment that does not always support an outward expression of loss, or understand that men are experiencing a painful sense of bereavement, elements of men's grief can go underground, leaving a confusing trail for those who do not know how to look for more. This issue figures in the loss of any significant relationship, including an animal companion.

Disenfranchised grief

Until recently, few mental health workers paid any mind to the psychological significance of animal companions in our lives. There is the story of psychologist

Boris Levinson, the father of modern animal-assisted therapy, who, in the 1960s, argued for the importance of the human-animal interaction to his colleagues at the American Psychological Association convention, only to be nearly laughed out of the meeting. The trickle-down effect of old notions still influences some therapists' perspectives when their clients discuss an animal companion. The temptation is to label this topic as unimportant or solely symbolic of some other loss from the past. In other words, losing an animal companion has not always been recognized widely as significant, and, in the worst situations, neither has it been taken seriously or seen as valid.

The more outdated points of view within the mental health profession also set a tone within popular culture, and how it understands loss. These are some of the notions I wish to address by writing this book. Without continuing efforts in many areas, the loss of a canine companion can lead to disenfranchised grief.

Disenfranchised grief is a significant loss that is not understood or recognized as legitimate.[2] Grief researcher Ron Niemeyer suggests that it is a failure of understanding at the cultural, familial, and personal levels regarding bereavement.[3] For mourners, the result is to withdraw from the outside world, not allowing others into the private world of grief for fear of further misunderstandings. The net effect is that personal material becomes even more locked away from view. Sometimes, if the missteps

of others are taken to heart, it may even make us question the legitimacy of our own reactions: "Am I making too much of this?"

Research on men's grief with human companions suggests that they are, on average, less likely to receive sympathetic responses, though are at the same time still expected to provide supportive gestures to others.[4] It could be that some believe men are not affected by loss as much, because they are taught to be tough, or the grief that is present goes unrecognized. It is not a big leap to expect similar outcomes when a man loses his canine companion.

I remember at the beginning of my career working with a middle-aged man who had a number of significant life concerns prompting him to come to therapy. In one of the sessions he looked away while mentioning that his dog had recently died. After sharing this fact, he glanced directly back at me for just a moment, his eyes began to water, and he seemed uneasy about the personal disclosure that had unintentionally slipped out. He understandably wondered how I would respond. I told him that this was a very significant loss. He sat quietly for a moment before saying, "Yes, it was. I didn't know if it was okay to bring it up." We spent the rest of the time talking about his dog, and how he had lovingly buried him in his backyard. He told me he dug the space slowly, taking breaks to think about the best memories of his friend.

That would not be the last time I encountered hesitancy about discussing the death of an animal companion, but the concern always seemed to be very similar: would it be taken as seriously as it was felt? Men's expression of loss may be confusing when filtered through the limits of traditional male socialization. While it places an emphasis on restricting outward displays of emotionality, feelings still may appear in fleeting moments, waiting to be acknowledged by someone who cares.

Society as a whole may not fully comprehend, and even a well-meaning friend or family member who knows that an animal companion was important may not grasp the exact reasons why one grieves. Again, this is another situation that does not help facilitate the grief process. However, the entire burden of appreciating the significance does not rest on others. There is an importance to becoming better skilled at exploring and expressing the words to tell our own stories. It is also means holding fast to the sense of legitimacy that rightfully accompanies the loss of *any* significant loved one.

Challenges in understanding men's grief about animal companions

The research examining male attachment to animal companions, and the intensity of grief when they are lost, is a work-in-progress, and what one might find in most textbooks and journals remains unclear. Some studies suggest that boys and men show lower levels of attachment, and fewer signs of sorrow, while others find no gender differences.[4]

Part of the problem with this line of investigation is that, until recently, few studies also considered the influence of traditional male socialization on how men answer such questions.[5] After all, making personal inquiries about tender feelings of any kind is counter to much of the old-style ways of enacting masculinity, and asking how men feel about their dogs can be one of them. Researchers can sometimes expect a biased or defensive response, when it seems someone is poking around in what feels like an intrusive way. Some males may deem this information to be off-limits to discuss. I have seen this issue firsthand in collecting surveys for my work about men and the bond. I sometimes get angry emails from online participants who filled out a questionnaire asking, "Why are you asking such ridiculous questions that have no relevancy?" Other times, when I have passed out the surveys in person at dog parks, some men will return the clipboard with the forms attached, and angrily refuse to participate stating, "It's none of your damn business."

While extreme examples are few and far between, some hesitancy is not. It can seem like a violation of stringent male norms regarding personal privacy. The potential influences beginning to shape tentativeness about discussing the bond start at a young age.

In one study examining the levels of attachment to their animal companions felt by boys and girls, as measured through the likelihood of expressing love to them, saying they were loved by them, and reporting missing them when apart, boys showed significantly lower levels of verbalizing these sentiments than girls.[6] The researchers concluded that male socialization seemed to have influenced boys' willingness to report their real feelings. When examining the actual behaviors shown toward their animal companions, no gender differences were found. At its heart, talking about the bond for boys or men involves tender feelings, ones that can seem off-limits for discussion.

Research from the past leaves many with the impression that all men don't grieve the loss of an animal companion as much, or on average perhaps do not feel all that attached in the first place, and part of my motivation for writing this chapter is to correct these mistaken conclusions, allowing for a more accurate picture of the deep connection between man and dog. So, asking a national sample of American men about their attitudes and behaviors in regard to grief and their animal companions also means inquiring about their perspectives on gender roles. I want to mention a few results from the nationwide survey I conducted when working on this book, about men's experience of losing an animal companion.

A significant majority of men (about 85 percent) endorsed the notion that the loss of their dogs was like losing a close friend or family member. This intensity is very consistent with others who describe losing animal companions that they felt attached to and loved. Likewise, men expressed the loss in a mix of heart and head grieving styles. Certainly, some men in the survey favored the more private, introspective forms of head grieving, while others expressed grief through "crying," and "feeling depressed." One additional emotional reaction also featured for almost a third of men – "A great deal" of "anger." The anger-funneling strategy mentioned earlier is important for some men when grieving an animal companion.

Given the significant place animal companions occupy for the majority of men, it was not surprising that the duration of grief was on a par with the bereavement period known to be associated with the loss of a human significant other or family member ("6-12 months"), although some reported that grief occasionally reappeared for years. Again, all of these responses are similar with those who value the bond in a special way. For those men who endorsed more traditional male norms – especially those who felt a need to restrict emotional expression – there was an expectation that others would not comprehend their loss, leading to an increased sense of disenfranchised grief. A quarter of men felt that, "Other people would not understand how I feel." This finding underscores how a significant number of men feel alone when working through the loss of their dogs. What remains unclear is how much these same men actually under-reported the intensity of what they felt about their animal companions.

What stands out for me from these research findings is that men do not necessarily love their dogs more or less than others; animal companions have the potential to take on a different meaning in men's lives. If men have smaller social networks, then those who are counted on within them carry heavier emotional connotations, and are sorely missed when gone. While acknowledging needing someone goes against much of traditional male socialization, saying that this same someone left a giant hole inside because they passed away can seem like a step too far for a number of men. But those who do talk about the experience of loss, whether through research surveys, sharing with a significant other, or sometimes in my office as a client, do so with a sentiment that could best be described as pure grief.

Pure grief is the parallel version of pure love; a grief that is absent of ambivalence and inconsistency. There are no mixed feelings toward one's animal companion who has been lost, just a sense of mourning that is untainted and clear. It always strikes me how someone unmistakably feels when talking about a lost loved one from the pure grief perspective. Sometimes, when working with men, there are just a few additional layers to peel back in order to see it.

The meaning of the lost bond

Understanding grief in the masculine world is not just about how sadness is expressed, but also about some of the barriers men may encounter in actually working through loss. Whether

in regard to losing a human or animal companion, men may not be primed to understand why someone was so special. There are not many traditional male seminars when growing up that teach us to think in those terms, and I believe this is one of the main reasons why, on average, men take longer to recover from losses such as divorce, or are more likely to remarry quicker after losing a significant other, or why almost a third of men grieving the loss of an animal companion in my survey felt that their best strategy for making the loss easier was to, "Put the whole thing out of my mind." The tools that would help process the grief fully are not always made available in men's socialization. Instead, males are taught to be 'Master and Commander' of our environment and emotions. This can include pressure to only be an instrumental griever.

Doka and Martin suggest that head grievers return to their jobs and their previous levels of performance sooner than heart grievers.[7] On paper, that would appear to be an approach consistent with traditional male socialization. It might even prompt some dog owners to move on to the next animal companion as the most viable solution. However, there is a danger in misreading 'taking action' as being the same as fully processing the deeper, symbolic meaning of the loss and having done all the necessary grief work. With head grieving alone, there is the issue of premature problem-solving when the loss is substantial. Simply attempting to set things back in place does not ensure that life and the deeper parts of our inner world also follow suit. The connection with various types of significant others, including an animal companion, form the core of who we are. Yet, how to determine their place in our lives may seem less tangible, something not easily assigned a numerical value or entered in a spreadsheet report. Their loss can even start a journey of deeper understanding about priorities, a re-examination of long-held beliefs, and discovery of our own place in the world.

The process of dealing with the aftermath of significant loss can be likened to a house in need of repair after a storm.[8] If only a couple small parts need fixing, the basic structure can stay in place, and it is essentially the same house with some minor cosmetic changes. In this case, a sense of consistency is maintained with the pre-existing viewpoints that were created before the loss.

However, when a tornado is significant enough to rock the structure, the house literally collapses, and new ways of supporting the belief systems need to be put in place. These are more than surface changes; they affect the foundation of the dwelling, sometimes making it necessary for the house to be rebuilt from the ground up.

The challenge with this scenario is much more labor-intensive, involving re-examining core values in order for the loss to be accommodated into one's sense of meaning. This includes resorting or expanding opinions, and possibly modifying one's identity.

Who a person is can literally change in the process.

Psychologist Ron Neimeyer suggests that when loss or death occurs, especially in an unexpected or violent way and seemingly for no good purpose, it can cause uncertainty about previously held assumptions that the world is predictable.[9] Instead, it seems random, dangerous, or unjust. However, even when death is non-violent, it can challenge a person's core beliefs. A protracted and painful illness that claims the life of a loved one may also cause the bereaved to question if the world is indeed safe or fair. The survivor may begin a chain reaction of re-examining once deeply held assumptions: "I will have to face my own mortality one day." "How much control is there really in life?" "Do people really get what they deserve?" "Is there an afterlife?" etc. The griever may, in turn, set out on a quest for new meaning(s). The most fundamental questions are asked, "Who am I really?" and "What does all this mean?"

Neimeyer says that regardless of whether or not a minor update or a major overhaul to one's personal sense of meaning and beliefs is needed, there is an attempt to resolve the inconsistencies that do not make sense any more after the experience of significant loss. While not every loss will trigger the need for a drastic re-examination, not embarking on re-sorting one's personal perspective when this *is* needed is associated with complicated grief reactions, and an identity that no longer makes sense. Sometimes, the griever has to go back through his or her life story, line-by-line, chapter-by-chapter, making updates and altering important events with the new perspective in mind. Loss can be such a powerful eye-opener that it's sometimes not possible to ever go back to some of the previously held viewpoints. This may be especially true if the pre-loss beliefs were actually at odds with each other, a bit flimsy, or maybe part of an inherited family legacy, seeing the world in a tacitly agreed upon way. For some, these views were adopted to survive the difficulty of growing up. Sometimes, these are the fabrications we tell ourself, because the real truth is too painful or confusing to be revealed.

Understanding the meaning of the bond in men's lives is no small undertaking. If the connection held a place of importance, or was lost through difficult means, this can cause us to re-examine long-held perspectives and our sense of personal meaning. In some cases, it even leads to the revision of our deepest beliefs: I know it did for me.

Midway upon the journey of my life

I am forty-nine years old. My wife, who is eight years younger, and has heard me go on about my age before, reminds me in a calm voice, "That is not that old ..." Yet, some mornings, I feel like I have an extra fifteen to twenty years of mileage. Even with those additional years, I can again hear her voice in my head say – this time in a less patient way – "That is not *that* old!"

Maybe the thing I am trying to work out is the heaviness that I sometimes feel. These days it is about extra wear and tear on my physical being. Unexpected and drawn-out health issues due to Meniere's disease, a condition that impacts balance and hearing, had me wondering if I might be trading in my psychology shingle for a long stint on disability. I began developing symptoms just a month after Kelsey passed away. The worst part lasted for about six years, leaving me with one functional ear that does its best in a very quiet environment. Otherwise, my speech recognition is not too good.

When I first started losing my hearing, I thought, for a short time, that I had been bestowed a sort of trade-off. I began noticing people in the public sphere say the most outlandish things. I thought, well, this is an ironic twist of fate: a psychologist who is becoming hearing-impaired can now discern people's true inner motives; ones not easily known before. I was disappointed to realize that this was not the discovery of a previously unrealized super power, and that I was usually just mishearing, or projecting onto others my own irreverent thoughts.

There are also equilibrium complications as the result of a malfunctioning balance organ that had to be removed. It sent messages to my brain that I was spinning in circles, even when I was perfectly still. It is kind of like the game of bat spin from childhood: put your forehead to the flat part of the bottom of a baseball bat, spin around it as many times as you can, and then try to run straight. Most of us just fall right over or feel pinned to the ground. There were a number of years of uncontrolled bat spins, vertigo, nausea, vomiting, and feeling pinned to the ground. My body had to adjust to various medications, surgeries, and rehabilitation, leading to changes in balance, some of which are still in process. When I walk down the long hall to my office I stare at a fixed point. When need be, I also drag my fingers down the wall, like a skier trying to find his edge going downhill. There are other lingering side effects, such as migraines, ringing in my ears, and fatigue. This is not the manliest self-disclosure, but I do my best when I shut my eyes for a few minutes between classes or clients.

All the physical issues began happening during a time that pre-dated my wife and her calm voice reminding me, "That is not that old." It was also a period marked by other life transitions and more losses. The heaviness I felt back then had a different name, and it was called grief. I can look back now with a somewhat sardonic chuckle, a way to achieve distance from what I could not back then, like I am part of a late-night TV skit, something akin to Monty Python or *Saturday Night Live.*

Knock, knock.

Who is it?

Life's Transitions, I have a delivery.

I didn't order any life transitions. You must have the wrong address.

Sorry, sir, but most people say the same thing. After all, who wants these? And I see you have several packages to be delivered. I will check them off as I read down the list. Let's see, a recent relationship ending, check; well, well, still a bachelor at your age; changes in health and well-being, check; employment change, check; geographic transition, check. Sir, I also see you are a dog lover; sorry to have to add the loss of an animal companion as well, check.

Well, it is really not a good time; can you bring those transitions back later? I am in the middle of a mid-life existential crisis.

Sorry, sir, there is a no return label on the packages. If you do not accept delivery, I will need to leave them outside your front door for you to sort out later. Either way, I believe some type of grief is in order.

I had read about grief, and certainly experienced it before, but there was something different about this time that made me lose my way. The 13th century poet Dante begins his poem "The Inferno," about one man's trip to the underworld, with these words, "Midway upon the journey of my life I found myself within a forest dark, for the straightforward pathway had been lost to me …"[10] When I reflect upon this passage, as so many middle-aged men have done before me, a straightforward path now being lost represents a turning point, a potential change of direction, which may occur at mid-life. Needless to say, this is not an easy change of course. The culmination of what

I thought life was supposed to be and what it was not began to disorient me, and I unexpectedly wandered lost into the woods. When I make the statement about things not being the way I had hoped, even counted on, I am sure there is some hint of a petulant child embedded within. However, there is also something more at work.

I have not always been a great believer in human beings. I want to be, but sometimes I am still not. When I was a boy, my father and I would have these discussions about humanity. In his more jaded moments, he felt strongly that people were not worth the investment. I, on the other hand, either through sheer reflex, or a son's need to prove his father wrong, took the opposing point of view. The thing is, back then, neither my father nor I brought to the table the direct implications of our conversations for the species in question, a species to which we both belonged. Not investing in humans had repercussions for my father's worth, my worth, and the eventual ways in which I would preserve hope that maybe good connections could eventually come along.

Psychoanalyst Ronald Fairbairn was among the first to emphasize how important it is for a child growing up to believe that there are good people in the world, ready and able to make connections.[11] These experiences form the cornerstone for the eventual conviction that goodness does exist, without which, all hope is lost.

Finding good attachments is so crucial that a child will go to great lengths to ensure that they actually do exist. It might include denying that things are so bad. Some even carry the 'burden of badness,' absorbing all that is wrong, so as to leave their caregivers shiny and faultless. The boy thinks: if only I am a better son, student, or athlete, I can win my caregiver's love. They are ready to give it to me and want me to have it. I just have to prove that I am worthy. In this way, even a child in tough circumstances can feel some sense of control over finding love and satisfying connections. These mental gymnastics involving self-blame are done in order to keep hope alive. Maybe one day, a different type of relationship will come along that does not have to be propped up, one strong enough to stand on its own merit. Until that time, the old conflicts get tucked away, and even a grown man will continue to operate under faulty childlike assumptions about how to prove that some semblance of good exists in the world, amid inevitable disappointments.

The circumstances set in motion by struggles with early attachment issues influenced me both in the formative years and then later when I grew up. It was no accident that, as a child, I began thinking of myself as an honorary member of a different species, one who walked on four legs instead of two. If I could form a bond here, there was the possibility that canine companions could carry me on their backs until I found my footing, and hope could be preserved. It was also no coincidence that I ended up in the helping profession, spending many years of training with the conflict about what to do with people tucked deeply in the back of my mind.

Even in my specialty area, working with men seemed preordained. Although my father often had a world-weary take on people, he still represented the more viable of my two parental attachment figures. My best memories of him are ones when he was supportive and encouraging. If I could save him in a symbolic way by helping men through my work, maybe I could be saved, too.

In some ways, I have been preparing to know more about the place where man meets dog all my life. Except now, these were not topics found on parallel roads that I viewed from an academic distance; they were ones that intersected in the middle of my own life. The effect made me turn further inward in an attempt to reconcile inconsistencies that had not so easily co-existed.

While I like to think that there has always been a part of me that believed in the magic of finding our better selves, that aspect got bent some as a child, or maybe it always was, under the weight of trying to preserve hope that good people did exist in the world. Sometimes, it led to being too demanding of myself, viewing disappointments only through the lens of not doing enough. Also, as I grew up, and close relationships either did not work out or died on the vine, it began to leave the impression that human connections were at best transient in nature.

Compare that with the day-in, day-out bond I had with my animal companions. They showed up every day. Once dogs love you, they always love you. They were a tangible presence, something that could be held onto, while ties with people were more ethereal; hard to grasp, waiting to float away, or me to walk away. As an adult, it seemed far safer and clearer to view my human connections from a distance, or at least that's what I thought.

Complicating these old patterns was my understanding of what being a man meant: being self-sufficient and comfortably alone. In the long run, the approach I am describing only fed my more avoidant tendencies. I needed a different type of connection, one that broke through the usual barriers and was able to reset some of the out of date and out of sync perceptions and approaches. Only then could a real belief in good connections truly come on-line. In either case, tightly-wound aspirational goals of finding good in the world, and even avoidant coping skills can only be stretched so far. The transitions and losses experienced in adulthood will open up old packages once stored away, forcing us to face what we have been running from.

In the novel *The Sense of An Ending*, British author Julian Barnes uses the narrative voice of his protagonist, a progressively aging middle-aged man, to convey the notion that relationships can be considered as a type of mathematical formula.[12] While successful ones can add to or multiply our experiences, failed ones can subtract from or divide them. Barnes notes there is the problem of 'accumulation:' after a lifetime of struggle or less-than-satisfying experiences, we can be left with a zero sum gain or, in the worst situation, insolvable personal algorithms.

I would argue that the ambiguity of accumulation is particularly troubling for men, and leaves us adrift, wanting – and perhaps needing – a bond that is instead both simple and pure. If such a connection can be found, it acts as a counterbalance, allowing for the possibility of new beginnings. It allows hope to be preserved.

When I lost Kelsey, I lost hope for a while. To me, she represented the most reliable goodness in the world, something I had been searching for all my life. I thought it existed apart from her at times, but it never entirely took hold. As you can imagine, the transition to making it on my own did not sit well with me. I was angry. I did not love my fellow man. I heard a voice from the past – one that I had previously captured and kept somewhat at bay, and now suddenly set free – say "I told you so." This led to what they refer to in the psychology textbooks as grief work. But engaging in it came at a risk, as it meant unleashing the possibility of not one layer of loss, but many, some old and some new. It also meant facing pain, confusion, ... and becoming a different sort of man.

Whereas avoidant themes had previously been present, in this period of my life, they took on a new level and meaning. I withdrew from others. My physical symptoms had worsened to the point of spending several hours resting for every one hour outside of my house. When I did try to engage others, it was frustrating. I could not reliably hear what they were saying, and did not want to start a conversation with someone I did not know with a litany of complaints, beginning with, "I lost a lot of my hearing recently, and I cannot understand you."

Having only limited contact with other people opened up a lot of time on my own, and, thankfully, with Sadie. It was when our twice-a-day walk ritual began, some with better levels of success than others. Given that a several hundred acre park was located just down the street, a portion of each morning and evening was spent moving slowly through the woods. On those hikes, Sadie did not seem to mind that I could not hear well, at best walked at a leisurely pace, or sometimes needed to sit down because I was experiencing vertigo.

As the treks went further into a forested area, I usually went deeper inside myself, thinking about issues of loss, Kelsey, and my place in the world. There was a mix of striving to make things better and the sometimes ineptness of passive despair. I struggled to get even the smallest amount of traction.

Some of the hardest parts of the grief work were aided by the expansiveness of nature around me. It was large enough to contain all that I felt, drawing out the sharpness and reshaping it as something else for a few moments. I tried to hold onto these flashes of understanding, gentleness, and catharsis. Being there in the woods was also a reminder that, while my problems were significant on a personal level, the rocks and trees had seen many others pass through countless times before.

I walked carefully in these thoughts, trying not to re-enact one of my mother's favored ways of offering support which did anything but – "If you feel sorry for yourself, find someone worse off." This involved trying to find a perspective that did not move to either extreme: despondency or total invalidation of the importance of my own sense of loss.

In more self-pitying moments, I also felt angry and defiant. There were times on these expeditions into grief when the woody canopy opened up, and I would shake my fist at the sky, daring something else to happen. "What else have you got?!" The thing I learned about loss is if important aspects feel stripped away by some other external force, whether that be God, life, loss, etc, there is the expectation that an outside power should also set it right. This sets up a painful waiting game, one where I looked for some action to occur on my behalf, a grand gesture allowing things to right themselves. Life, of course, does not really work like that, operating on the childish demands of perceived fairness. Making matters worse in these moments were other personal liabilities.

In the best instances, I am a persistent person. This quality has helped in a number of ways in my life, but there is a temptation for that characteristic to become lopsided under extreme duress, making me a very stubborn and

willful man. In these cases, a manufactured and groundless hope of getting what I thought I deserved was a dangerous thing. So I camped outside the metaphoric home office and waited, occasionally banging on the door, demanding some justice, and I was not moving until I got it.

What I slowly began to realize was that my approach was not only fruitless, but also part of the problem of being mired in grief. I could not remake the people who were important to me into different versions, especially not by stubbornly holding my breath until they changed. Nor could I count on Kelsey showing up in those woods, joining Sadie and me on a walk. Even with things like health issues, sometimes they have to run their course. In the meanwhile, I had to set things right as much as I could from the inside, which actually could help make a new course for different opportunities on the outside. It meant I had to be an active player, sidestepping my own limits.

With each return from these sojourns in the forest, I remember having the distinct impression that I was getting thinner, losing one layer after another of who I was, until I imagined myself a skeleton of my former self. Some strata I wanted to be free from, such as childhood sadness, familial misperceptions, and old issues that tainted various areas of my life. These included the notion that previously experienced losses and letdowns were always somehow the result of me not doing enough. While it gave the illusionary sense of control as a child, I was not a boy any more. Revisiting these themes came at a cost, as they had grown into and wrapped themselves around me. Pulling them loose felt sharp, sometimes making me recoil.

I used to take grief out like a sculptor working on a yet-to-be-formed piece of stone. I cannot say what it was supposed to be, what shape it was to take. I just carved, chipped, sometimes banged, and occasionally placed my fist through it. Sometimes I cursed what I felt, swearing that I would never touch it again, and not let it touch me. But whether walking in the woods with Sadie or not, it eventually found me, and I found it, and some mornings back then, I felt heavier, like I was older than I was.

But as I worked on it, it was also working and changing me, sometimes in slow, steady ways, and other times in sharp, rough ones. What I did not realize was that I was still trying to find a way to believe. At the bottom of grief was a switch that, when successfully flipped, would allow me to move beyond simple explanations which no longer served their purpose. I had outgrown self-blaming justifications like a jacket that no longer fit, but I did not want to spend the rest of my life as a disillusioned curmudgeon, either, seeing no good in the world. I was searching for a bond that would allow faith to be restored. Believing is the middle-aged man's salvation; it rekindles hope.

But even self-reliant men are not self-sufficient. We need someone to provide the inspiration, and sometimes guidance to accomplish the task. Even Dante had a Virgil as a guide, helping him negotiate "The Inferno." Some men find the vital qualities in the innocence of their children or grandchildren; others through the love of their wife or a close friend. Other men are gripped by the steadfast loyalty and trustworthiness of a canine companion. A dog can help a man who is lost in the darkness find his way. I know this is where Kelsey's memory helped sustain me, and was the relational foundation upon which I built. As I found a new type of bond with her after she passed, I also discovered a more genuine belief in connecting with at least a few others.

Sadie was one of those connections that helped me come back from the middle-aged underworld. She was the single most reliable bond I had for several years, which, in some ways, she still is today. One example of that dependability was her uncanny ability to recognize when I was about to have a Ménière's episode.

Part of the drill to ward off hours of vertigo and throwing up was catching it early enough, and then staying absolutely motionless for an extended period of time. As I was doing this, I would break into cold sweats and try to will the ceiling back from its cyclone-like appearance. During this time, Sadie would jump up on the bed and hunker down right by my side. On the occasions I was not able to catch the spins soon enough, I would begin the ritual. It was like the vertigo had become affixed to the muscles in my diaphragm, and needed to be worked out to absolute exhaustion, never one episode of sickness, but many. I would pass out on the bathroom floor or with my head in the toilet. When I eventually opened my eyes and turned my head, Sadie would be there. Later, when I met the woman who became my wife, her presence was another that tugged at me to rejoin the world of the living. She also got infused into the preventive Ménière's routine: me lying on the bed, Sadie on one side of me and Lora on the other. I felt sandwiched between their care.

There were many reasons for undertaking the journey, understanding what the bond between man and dog means and why, but the one I am sharing now reflects deeper motivations, which I did not know were fully at play in my life. I had to find a continuing bond with Kelsey. I really had no choice. There was so much at stake. While some may resonate with this part of my story, I also realize that a new type of bond with someone who has passed is sought for different reasons, some of which we may be more aware of, and other parts are revealed in time. It took many years to uncover the many motivations driving me forward.

Shortly after finishing this part of the grief work expedition, I had a dream about Kelsey. We were on the road, as we often were when I was in graduate school, staying at a travel motel. It was a sunny morning, and the air was fresh. I stepped outside the room onto the green lawn of the courtyard. I saw Kelsey at a distance and called her name. She came running to me, easily negotiating the potential water hazard between us of a badly-placed swimming pool. Kelsey then stood in front of me as

she had in her prime, wagging her tail, tongue hanging out, catching her breath. She gave me a smile. I cannot put into words what it was like to see her again this way. She had such vital energy. Seeing her also stirred in me something I thought the heaviness of grief had permanently claimed. A part of me was brought back to life in that moment, our bond helping me find my way.

I do not want to be a child again with childlike perspectives of the world, people, or myself. Instead, I am after reasonable outlooks on important matters. Yes, there are disappointments, and, yes, there are losses, but there are also attachments with those who are steady and can be counted on. This is not an either/or proposition, though some part of me was tempted to believe it had to be for so long. What I experienced lays down tracks for a new and different way. It is a fought-for perspective that attempts to shun naiveté and deal with the ambiguity that is a part of living. It means revisiting my motivations for the work I do and the attachments I seek. While I am not immune to frustration, both seem less pressured now, and freer from the dire consequences that once loomed over me if things did not go as planned. Both can take on a different dimension that is not cloaked in the shadow of my fears. Instead, they can be something else, perhaps the thing that they are meant to be, a nuanced and more grown-up understanding made possible by bonds that reignited the flame of hope.

There are moments when I feel this hope, and it is

overwhelming. Its strength and purity seems to leap up from deep inside. My voice cracks and my eyes moisten. In these moments, I find a way to allow the petty grievances about life to be put to one side, and the better part of me comes forward. In these instances, I can offer encouragement, because I feel it. What is not evident is its source: a dog named Kelsey and another called Sadie, and a small circle of others that have come to know the reasons why both my animal companions are so important.

Do men fundamentally grieve in a different way, especially in regard to the loss of animal companions? I think what is most unique about the male experience is feeling blocked off from the wider range of ways to express grief for many significant losses. This hindrance is especially evident when the loss is someone who feels irreplaceable within the often-cramped quarters of a dwindling social network. Making matters worse, the tools are not always there to make sense of how that

bond touched our lives. Instead, many feel compelled to take only practical steps designed to get back to work. We miss out on the simple fact that bonding is a central part of that effort. At heart, though, men are fully capable of both loving and mourning; sometimes the skillsets just need to be broadened and deepened in an environment that feels safe.

The relationship with man's best friend plays a prominent role in many men's lives, but male socialization can block the needed efforts to discuss and understand their loss. Our animal friends help create a special place of connection rarely known by others, which allows some of our personal issues to be worked out, or at least provides a companion while wandering around, making sense of our inner landscape. This emotional space and the one who helps form it are not necessarily meant to be exclusionary by design. Rather, an animal companion helps many of us find the courage to reach out and invite someone else in.

Visit Hubble and Hattie on the web: www.hubbleandhattie.com
www.hubbleandhattie.blogspot.co.uk
• Details of all books • Special offers • Newsletter • New book news

7

Search and recovery – the continuing bond

But if the while I think on thee, dear friend,
All losses are restored and sorrows end.
– William Shakespeare; Sonnet 30

Once, a grieving mother went to the Buddha. She told him of the numerous losses she had experienced in her life, but none more poignant than the most recent one, that of her infant child. The Buddha listened patiently and had compassion for her. He said, "If you can find a home that has not known loss or death, we will find a way to bring your child back to life." With that, the grieving mother immediately set out upon her journey.

At first, the grieving mother moved from dwelling to dwelling, inquiring of each stranger she encountered, "Has this home known loss or death?" When the answer was invariably 'Yes,' she would dart on to the next residence without another word, often leaving the person in the doorway surprised or unsettled.

One day, she asked someone, "Has this home known loss or death?" When the grieving mother received the usual reply, she prepared to move on, but this time the person said, "Stop ... why do you ask such a question?" The grieving mother froze in her tracks. Tears began forming in her eyes, and she told her story. The person listened patiently with thoughtfulness and a sense of understanding that only knowing personal loss brings.

The next day, the mother continued on with her journey, stopping at the first dwelling she encountered on the road, and like so many times before, asking the person who answered the door, "Has this home known loss or death?" The grieving mother could tell by the person's reaction that she had known both, and, instead of turning to canvass another home, she listened to the other woman's story with empathy. Afterwards, realizing that every home has known some form of loss and death, the mother decided to return and study with the Buddha, and devoted her life to helping others work through their own sense of bereavement.

The notion that loss and death are inescapable can be difficult to accept. In fact, there is a recent shift in attitude toward the end of the life cycle with deliberate attempts to shield its very existence.[1] The current fluctuating nature of the modern family also reflects this discomfort. Once, it was common for multiple generations to live in the same home or nearby, so that, in a single broad stroke, one could witness the assortment of goings-on that occurred across a lifespan. This might include couples forging new relationships, newborns entering the world, individuals enjoying the prime of life, as well as those transitioning to the later years. But having multiple generations in or near one space has been replaced with a shrinking nuclear family, with those in different life stages partitioned off. Subsequently, more demands are made of those few connections in the inner circle (human and animal companions), and a pressure to not dwell on the happenings of our later years. Ultimately, the newer familial arrangement can make one feel as though the stakes are higher on many fronts, including preserving ties to those significant others, as well as shying away from difficult realities.

These days the complex and multilayered themes of life and loss may be more fully realized in the context of a relationship with an animal companion.[2] Many 'firsts' occur in the company of our dogs; other times, we play host to theirs. Even if it is condensed into a relatively short period of time, it is common for the full life cycle to be experienced with an animal companion: an all-encompassing experience that is rare by today's standards. For this reason alone, the bond between animals and people proves special.

Being in the presence of animal companions also allows other familial themes to arise. The point of connection between the generations can be at times our dogs; described by psychologists as a "social lubricant" that make awkward situations easier.[3] This might include welcoming the in-laws for a weekend stay at your cramped apartment, or when the conversation at Thanksgiving between estranged family members comes to a standstill. In each of these situations, an animal companion's presence can relieve tension and place everyone at ease. The power of the bond links many distinct happenings across our lifespan, including those which are sometimes the hardest to face.

Whether it involves human or animal companions, it makes sense that there is sometimes a need to compartmentalize loss and death, keeping both at a safe distance. The events can feel unfamiliar and overwhelming. At the same time, keeping things completely removed can lead to a disconnection from the last phase of life, and with it the development of erroneous assumptions or skewed points of view. Some may feel like characters in a child's morality play or fairytale. Only those who transgress some social more must face these realties; everyone else lives as they are now, happily ever after.

As adults, it can be tempting to carry forward this naïve mentality when contemplating a natural, though sometimes difficult, part of living. That is, until loss is encountered firsthand, and with it the wondering, "How can this be? I am a good person, citizen, and significant other. Shouldn't I be protected from loss?" Some will assume that loss is the rightful punishment for our sins. Others will hope for immunity through some type of perceived status, affiliation, or set of beliefs. They conclude that this must be a mistake and, much like the grieving mother with the Buddha, feel compelled to find a loophole.

Confronted with the inevitability that every home has known loss or death, where do we go? The challenge involves finding life after loss and, with it, updating some of the antiquated notions of grieving.

This chapter focuses on the search for and recovery of a bond with someone who has died. The process of building what is referred to as a 'continuing bond,' and examples of how some accomplish this new type of connection, are explored. The approach has direct relevance to the loss of animal companions.

The ties that bind

Psychoanalyst Sigmund Freud provided an interesting metaphor for how attachments form, one that would often be used in dealing with loss.[4] When making an emotional investment in another, it is like creating an emotional tether to them. Each strand of connection is derived from a memory, an event, and a significant time that deepened the relationship. Over the course of the relationship, these experiences literally bind us together, forming the basis for a bond. The greater sense of shared history often leads to more ties with those who are loved. However, when someone special is lost, there is the problem of what to do with all the tethers.

Freud's pragmatic solution was that one needed to sever all ties to the departed, cutting the tethers one by one, thereby freeing emotional energy that could then be reinvested elsewhere in new relationships. Freud placed an emphasis on how grieving in theory returns one to a pre-loss level of functioning. Likewise, some subsequent psychoanalytic writers and grief experts have argued that it is necessary to break all bonds with the departed in order to complete bereavement.[5] If feelings or memories still linger, these are signs the required work has not been finished. In fact, the old model held that the remaining connections with the departed should be viewed in more pathological terms if they persisted beyond helping one eventually let go. The clearing-out-of-the-metaphoric-closet approach usually leaves no remnants of the past, including all the good things associated with the bond. If this is our stance, it can feel even more compelling to be a home that has known neither loss nor death.

While Freud offered his early conceptualization of grief work as a tentative theory that needed further exploration, for many years aspects of it remained as the prevailing word on what it meant to grieve. However, Freud would later revisit his earlier work after many painful losses of his own.[6] He had undergone more than thirty cancer-related operations, had seen the passing of his closest daughter, Sophie, and later his four-year-old grandson, and had become estranged from a number of heir apparents within the psychoanalytic inner circle. His remaining daughter, Anna, whom he came to rely on heavily, was growing more independent, professionally and personally. He also had to flee his home in Vienna because of mounting political issues that led to World War II. Through that pre-war period, he even temporarily relied on others for financial assistance. In the midst of these various losses, especially were family members; Freud confided to a friend that he believed himself incapable of loving again. It was in the later part of his life when he would eventually find some relief in the company of his animal companions.[7]

For many years already, Freud had had a special connection with animals, especially dogs. He and his daughter, Anna, would even write birthday rhymes and poetry to one another in the guise of their family German Shepherd. But in the midst of loss, his animal companions took on a new, special role, and Freud was able to derive some comfort from canine companionship. Michael Molnar, former Research Director at the Freud Museum in London, noted that the man-canine relationship manifested in a number of ways.[8] Freud was often photographed traveling with one of his Chows, and his dog was omnipresent in his consultation room as he saw patients. Freud, who now wore a prosthetic jaw as the result of cancer, even made good use of his dog's canine teeth on his behalf at meals, allowing her to masticate his meat so he could eat it.

Freud wrote about his personal journey of grief in letters to friends and colleagues, confessing how his own bonds to loved ones could neither be relinquished nor replaced.[9] At the same time, he felt unable to maintain a continuing connection with those he loved and lost, sinking into a deep depression, attempting to face such matters with stoicism. The tragedy was he could explain the inner workings of the mind brilliantly, but was unable to find a workable solution to life after loss.

The continuing bond

Finding a way to face grief is no easy task. But there has been a fairly recent shift from earlier assumptions that severing the bond with a lost loved one is what it means to achieve successful bereavement. Instead, there is an emphasis on maintaining a continuing bond.[10]

The continuing bond concept underscores an ongoing relationship with those who have died as a normal part of life after loss. There is the recognition that loss has occurred, and the usual means of connecting are no longer available. However, those seeking to sustain a connection learn to do so in various new ways, which are discussed in more detail later in the chapter. This shift in perspective toward grieving emphasizes how finding a new way to connect with a lost loved one is healthy, not a sign that mourning is still incomplete, or a reflection of some type of pathological bereavement. A continuing bond can even be a source of emotional and psychological support that adds much to our lives.

The continuing bond approach is also consistent with other cultures and traditions which remember or connect with the departed as a normal and regular part of living. This can be done in ritual form, as part of ceremonies, or even as the grieving mother did in the story with the Buddha: letting the remembrance be a motivating and positive part of everyday living. Whether the bond is made with a human or animal companion, the relationship with the lost loved one is reincorporated back into our life in a new way. While there may be no such thing as a house free from loss or death, there is comfort in knowing that a new type of relationship with those who have passed can be a healthy part of life after loss.

While the notion of the continuing bond has been voiced by a minority of scholars and clinicians for some time, it has often been overlooked.[11] Part of the reason for this lies with a distorted view of individuality in Western culture. According to this standpoint, being 'your own person' also means not really needing others, or a forced choice between significant bonds and one's individuality. The focus on hyper independence continues to rise, leaving many alone.

The American Sociological Review reports that the number of adult close friends is on the decline, with the most-often-reported number of close friendships in 1985 being three, dropping in 2004 to zero.[12] The percentage of adults who report having no close friends at all increased from 36 percent in 1985 to 53.4 percent by 2004. There is also a related gender issue to consider for males.

In the book, *Deep Secrets: Boys' Friendships and the Crisis of Connection.* Researcher Dr Niobe Way makes a poignant point that loneliness is seen as a necessary rite of passage for boys on the journey to manhood,[13] and argues that although boys actually want emotional intimacy, as they hit late adolescence, they feel a pressure to 'man-up' and go-it- alone.

Struggles dealing with attachment and loss are also linked to a distorted view of individuality, seen in the nature of throw-away relationships. By necessity, this entails letting them go in order to move on to greener pastures and personal fulfillment elsewhere. The idea of 'me' not being compatible with 'we' figures deeply in American mythos. One example includes the story of how the 'West was won' in the 19th century, emphasizing the rugged masculine individualist who tamed the frontier on his own.[14] The reality is that, in the best moments, it was actually accomplished by rugged individuals who were also part of a cooperative community.

In order to reorient to a new approach focusing upon a continuing bond, it is essential to discuss a related topic – searching.

Search and recovery

Grief experts claim that, when a loved one dies, initially, a person is of two minds. One part attempts to accept that the circumstances are painful, but real, while the other protests the loss.[15] The protest phase can be intense, fueled by the desire to maintain the tie in its original form. Various emotions – anger, frustration, and pining – push us forward through perceived and real barriers that keep us and the loved one apart: in essence, a search begins for them, fueling the hope of a possible reunion.

Pioneering grief expert Colin Murray Parkes argues that the mourner begins the search by constructing a mental map of familiar places, sights, and sounds related to the loved one.[16] By following the diagram and attending to its clues, there is the hope that, sooner or later, the loved one will turn up. One may hear the creak of a door opening, or familiar footsteps on a tiled floor, each resonance being an indication that the lost loved one will now appear, just as they did on so many previous occasions. There is a quick turn in anticipation, each tactile indication pointing toward the unmistakable scenario of separation giving way to reunion, thinking, even now, that we catch a glimpse of our friend, animal companion, or family member moving through the hallway.

Other times a certain object is cradled with gentle care, one that carries special meaning, evoking memories of the past. There is a wish that this item has somehow been transformed into a talisman, carrying extraordinary powers to bring back the dead. The search may even occur within the netherworld of dreams, the depository of unvoiced thoughts and emotions.

The problem with the mental map that has been painstakingly constructed is that it is ultimately flawed. Yes, the coordinates do indicate the correct location of once-familiar meeting places, and, under normal circumstances, the loved one being desperately sought would eventually turn up. However, these are not the usual conditions; and, at best, there is an intermittent moment of hope that is followed each time only by frustration. The search can have remnants of the most raw and intense protest occurring in childhood when separated from caregivers, at one time the most effective tool in terms of facilitating a reunion. If one pines long and loud enough, the special someone who is the object of our tender despair will soon relieve us from the burden of separation. There is evidence for searching in many types of bonds.

Searching for a lost companion

Ethnologist Konrad Lorenz is often pictured as an elderly

man walking around his college campus with baby graylag geese following him in procession. The geese had imprinted upon Lorenz, believing him to be their mother. He pioneered field research to better understand various facets of animals' lives, including how they attached, but also how they grieved. From his field observations in the wild, he noted that animals (mammal and non-mammal alike) showed signs of searching. Lorenz studied the occurrence among the graylag goose, a species that bonded deeply and mated for life. He observed the mournful call that occurred when mates were separated by death –

"The first response to the disappearance of the partner consists of the anxious attempt to find them again. The goose moves about restlessly by day and night, flying great distances and visiting places where the partner might well be found, uttering all the time the penetrating trisyllabic long distance call … The searching expeditions are extended farther and farther, and quite often the searcher itself gets lost, or succumbs to an accident … All the objective observable characteristics of goose behavior on losing its mate are roughly identical with human grief."[17]

Lorenz is not the only scientist to make note of the distinct and sometimes overwhelming urge for searching. More recently, evolutionary biologist Marc Bekoff remarked on the emotional lives of animals, and when grief takes center stage.[18] Instances reported by various scientists include a non-human animal's attempts to revive the corpse of a family member, or even carry it around until it decomposes. Sometimes, the story of searching can also involve how non-human animals search for their human companions.

There is the example of Professor Hidesaburō Ueno, and his dog, Hachikō. At the end of each workday, Hachikō greeted the professor at the nearby train station, and they would walk home together. The pair continued their daily routine for years, until the professor suffered a cerebral hemorrhage and died, never returning home to the train station where his friend was waiting. Each day for the next nine years, Hachikō appeared precisely when the train came that should be carrying the professor, and waited. He became a permanent fixture at the train station, which eventually attracted the attention of other commuters. His faithfulness to his master's memory brought nationwide notoriety. In 1934, a bronze statue in his likeness was erected at what is now known as 'The Hachikō Exit' at Shibuya Station.

When I share the story about Hachikō and the professor, I see my wife gets a little uncomfortable, and then I realize why. There is a good chance some version of Hachikō's story will also be how things will go if I pass away before Sadie. Sadie has always been a one-person dog. She gets noticeably distressed whenever I drag my travel carry-on bag out of the closet, and goes through a painful period of pining when I go away, usually not eating for the first day or so. The picture that stays in my mind is the parting shot. She sits by the doorway entrance looking out the side window as I leave, with a mournful look that is painful to bear, and my wife tells me that Sadie will stay there for hours, waiting for my return.

There are also instances of people searching for animal companions. John, a friend of mine, was also a horse whisperer of sorts, and had the ability to relate to equines in unique ways. Shortly after John passed, his wife shared with me a collection of short stories he had been working on for more than twenty years, as she thought they might help me with writing this book. The Xeroxed copy she gave me was of the original work, with lines crossed through sentences, queries about which was the best word to use in describing an experience, and, embedded within, a personal journey he had been taking since he was a boy.

The story was about his dog, Einer, an overzealous Greyhound who came to live with John's family after making his puppy debut on a sheep farm out west. The pages revealed the family mythology, including Einer's antics, which grew to legendary proportions. The boys in the neighborhood would do their version of the fast and the furious, drag racing against the dog. As the story goes, Einer never lost a race. Then there was the time Einer, prone to following the family around town, wandered into John's sister's college classroom. Being none too shy in terms of claiming his own, Einer found the young lady and laid down right beside her desk.

Perhaps the most difficult story involving Einer was about his disappearance. In fact, the title of the story is *Looking for Einer*, which John did for most of the rest of his life. There is a mix of details in John's notes as he plays detective, trying to reconstruct his dog's whereabouts. Did the man who herded sheep need Einer back to work on the ranch? Or did Einer's disappearance have something to do with the war (World War II), and money being in short supply? John never got a clear answer, but he never stopped searching for Einer, either. He was seventy years old and still trying to piece together the story, sometimes wondering if he might eventually run into someone who had heard of this amazing Greyhound.

I believe John eventually found Einer in essence; in part, through his many years of being a school counselor, trying to provide guidance for kids. He encouraged them to take a different path than he himself was tempted by in his youth. He also found Einer in his work with horses. John's horse, Vito was another adolescent of sorts who experienced release in his presence. I cannot help but think that somewhere in the back of John's mind, being with a horse who stood over sixteen hands tall was somehow reminiscent of how it must have been to be a small boy standing in the presence of a tall, lanky Greyhound big enough to ride. You see, everyone searches for their own version of Einer, and sometimes we just don't realize he has been found, mysteriously incorporated, without fully comprehending it, into the very fabric of our lives.

Whether discussing the concept of searching in regard to non-human or human animals, it seems indicative of a deeper truth that may easily become lost amid the shuffle of our lives. It involves our true nature as social creatures, needing to make and sustain a connection with at least one other. When a permanent separation occurs from those who are loved, it is innately distressing and disorienting, and the normal reaction is to seek a reunion. As human animals, the same searching sequence occurs when a pet who has transformed into an animal companion passes away. Just like with any other family member, our biological directive is activated to search and recover.

Overcoming loss: the continuing bond

Psychoanalyst John Bowlby believed it made sense that a search is conducted for a loved one after a loss out of sheer routine.[19] After all, separation-reunion is part of a predictable sequence in any long-term relationship. Reunions are counted on, and follow the many, many separations that occur over the course of any connection. However, to never come back together is an anomaly of epic proportions. A part of our personal history prompts us to hold the notion that all separations can be overcome. The pain of loss also pushes us forward in the search.

At first, the loved one is sought in familiar places with our old mental map. The supreme difficulty is that they cannot be found. The inevitable ineffectiveness of such a heartfelt quest now, after so many frustrations, allows the loss to become real. Even with acceptance it may not keep us from looking in new ways. Where one type of search ends, there is the potential for another to begin.

I am convinced that a second version of searching, when guided in the right way, will lead us to the goal. I am not talking about an illusory bond, or one that leaves us frozen in the past. Rather, it involves a continued relationship with the lost loved one, and with it, a continuing bond. The searcher recognizes that connecting will not occur in the way it once did, but is, nevertheless, a way to retain the connection, the memories, and all that was important. The bond becomes a permanent fixture upon which one can still viably rely. A continuing bond is applicable with both human and animal companions.

Recent research by Dr Wendy Packman and her colleagues has found a number of different ways a continuing bond is made with an animal companion.[20] In one study, a set of 12 different approaches were used in varying degrees by men and women grieving their loss –

- sense of presence
- use of belongings
- associated places
- fond memories
- dreams
- thoughts of being reunited with deceased
- living up to ideals or wishes
- everyday decisions
- reminiscences
- memorials

• intrusive symptoms
• lessons learned

The researchers also compared the same strategies with another group of mourners who were attempting to reform a connection with a lost human significant other. They concluded that the same basic process of forming a continuing bond occurred with both groups of mourners – those who lost an animal or a human companion. The most often utilized strategies were: "recalling fond memories," "holding onto or using belongings" of the lost loved one, "reminiscing with others," and thinking about "lessons learned/positive influences" gained from the special someone in their life. The majority of participants mourning the loss of an animal companion also said they often had thoughts and dreams of being reunited with their animal companion.

Besides how strikingly similar the approaches were in forming continued bonds with both animal and human companions, was the extent to which the continuing bond strategies brought comfort, and were also, at times, distressing.

It is important to recognize that a continuing bond is not a panacea or a firewall against all pain. For instance, it makes sense that, when recalling a cherished memory, some sense of satisfaction would occur. At the same time, maybe some frustration also occurs because that special someone is not around to make more. However, it was the case for both groups in Dr Packman's study that forming the continued bond was more often a source of comfort rather than pain.

The researchers also found that the more well-being one could draw from the continued bond, the more likely it was that the overall sense of grief would decrease. That speaks to a skillset learned in time, like building a new relationship with an old friend which will eventually allow their presence to be felt in a deeper way, thereby also bringing more comfort and ease.

One other finding to consider from Dr Packman's study is how, as the continued bond grew, grievers were also more likely to experience post-traumatic growth: a significant personal, positive change. This suggests that, even after their passing, an animal companion can still impact our lives in powerful ways, helping us become wiser, stronger, and kinder people. I want to highlight four continued bond approaches aligned with Dr Packman's research that I also found in my own nationwide survey of men and their animal companions.

Calling on the memory

One of the most common ways to form a continuing bond is through memories. Most of us have had the experience of thinking back to special times shared with a loved animal companion, allowing us to feel their presence in our lives. A slightly different take on this is actually calling on the memory of an animal companion. While one may stumble upon a cherished memory by sorting through the storage shed, or encounter a familiar theme while someone in the family watches Lifetime TV, it is important to know that actually calling on the memory when it is needed or desired is also an option. This is an active and willed choice.

Calling on the memory is also different from the intrusive type of remembering associated with painful recollection that is sometimes unbearable. Referring back to Dr Packman's research, one strategy that was used in trying to keep a connection going was related to 'intrusive symptoms.' This is an extreme version of being at the mercy of memories triggered by surroundings or seemingly stuck in the loop of remembering images and thoughts, and experiencing feelings. This can be similar to a haunting loss, where the mourner is unable to control memories about the lost loved one that are agonizing. There were a few men in my survey who mentioned this type of uncomfortable experience, and it was usually related to an unexpected, accidental, or violent end for their animal companion. One man mentioned that his dog was stabbed by a stranger, and the recollection intruded into his thoughts every day. Over time, many of us sort through intrusive thoughts of sadness, and instead are able to invite in the best memories. In special circumstances, this takes extra work.

Calling on the memory of an animal companion can evoke strong positive emotions. If those memories are gathered in our mind, and are developed clearly enough, it can feel as if a part of that special someone occupies a permanent place inside our minds.

It's like having a portable snapshot of the loved one accompany us on life's journey. In more psychological language, this is sometimes referred to as 'internalization' of the loved one. I know when I think of Kelsey I see in my mind's eye a familiar facial expression, one of her tongue-wagging smiles, with her green eyes aglow, and it never fails to brighten my day.

The called-upon image of an animal companion appears in many different scenarios, and is especially important when considering the various roles they once filled. In times past, turning to our friend could involve meeting a range of needs, including soothing us in difficult moments, and prompting us to respond to life's challenges in adaptive ways. Now that our companion is no longer here to perform the much-needed tasks, their memory helps us stretch and do them for ourselves. The image becomes a sort of lifecoach or moral compass that helps inspire ways to think, feel, and act. The memory may provide situation-specific guidance, or help clarify our perspectives on a range of circumstances and decisions. More than a few men discussed in my nationwide survey how calling on the memory acted as inspiration to be a better partner or parent, or when they found themselves at a difficult crossroads, it helped them decide what to do based on an animal companion's inspiration for a better life.

Sometimes calling on the memory of our animal companion is also done for a moment of togetherness. The image allows us to be warmed again by their presence in our lives. Some men did this, thereby initiating a visit as a way to mark special occasions, including the anniversary of the animal companion's passing. For others, their animal companions find their way into their dreams, where a moment of togetherness is experienced. Some men commented that they remember their animal companion in daily prayers or meditations, just as they would any other beloved family member who was no longer present, but still loved.

Memorial

Another key way to form a continuing bond is by making an external memorial. Sometimes it is easier to have something tangible that helps sustain the connection, and this can include old items that hold an unusual meaning, or new ones that bestow a symbolic quality. Each of these is a form of memorial. Certified grief therapist and animal behavior therapist Barbara Meyers noted that a memorial has a positive connotation, and is some type of physical monument commemorating the full range of experiences that have occurred.[21] A memorial enables us to experience the sum of the connection, and helps remake the new bond through an appeal to our tactile senses.

The solid and substantial memorial is different from a shrine. A shrine, by way of comparison, may pay homage to another, but does not recognize the fullness of experience, including the occurrence of loss. Instead, it tries to keep things exactly as they were before the bond was broken. A shrine cannot contain the complete range of our connection. It pushes us away from the realities of grief, loss, and also the continued bond.

Examples of how a memorial is utilized in forming a continued bond with an animal companion include pictures and mementos. Some men use a well-placed photo on their desk or fireplace mantel as a way to remember and reconnect.

There are also memorials that involve the senses in another way, such as a collar stored in an airtight bag allowing the remnants of the dog's scent to be preserved. On special occasions, one of the study participants would take it out and literally breathe in the connection of his old friend. Sometimes, plaster pawprints are used as a tangible reminder of the dog tracks that made an impression on our life. Tracing them with our fingers helps trigger memories of actual adventures shared. Others have created websites dedicated to their dog, or written a biography about their life, or posted an online obituary after working on it for a week or more. In one instance, a tree was placed alongside a new bench, both being near the final resting place of an animal companion. This created a special meeting place where the lost bond could be found. The memorial could also assume a larger scale, like a kennel, or even an orchard, bearing the name of our dog.

A memorial can also take the form of an annual ritual. One person in my survey bought a plastic pumpkin every Halloween, and kicked it around in remembrance of how he and his dog would play in the same way, creating their own version of trick-or-treat. One of the most heartwarming stories shared involved an elderly man and his beloved canine companion. On special occasions, including on the anniversary of his death, the man would go to his dog's resting place and hold a vigil, sitting, visiting, and taking a nap alongside his old friend. In each of these examples, a memorial becomes an external and tangible way to claim a continuing bond.

Community

A sense of community can also help with finding life after loss. This way of creating a continuing bond involves a network of friends and family. In other circumstances, it is a community consisting of just one other person, providing the much-needed space to reflect about experiences relating to our animal companion. Regardless of the size, community helps one bear the weight of loss by not being alone with the grief. Having someone to talk with is important in processing various aspects of grief, especially if, as mentioned above, the mourner feels blocked from forming a continued bond through intrusive sadness, guilt, or remorse. I was once on a plane working on this manuscript, and a fellow passenger inquired about the work.

After I'd explained, he responded by telling me the terrible self-reproach he felt for having to make a spilt-second decision in the vet's office about putting down his dog. The vet had told him that there was very little likelihood his dog would recover from the newly-diagnosed condition, and the man, wanting to spare his animal companion further suffering, decided to let him go, but at a great cost. The man had regretted his decision for years. With this type of situation, he, and others like him, need to share their concerns, thereby clearing away barriers to a continued bond.

When the community is particularly attuned to our needs, it begins to feel as though a world that was once impoverished by loss now becomes renewed through sharing reactions and hearing those of others. This dialogue allows memories to be passed back and forth, solidifying the story of the bond in a way that helps remake the connection. A well-intended listener can ask questions and act as a mirror for our own emotional reactions. We sometimes know our story better after sharing it in the presence of another. In various ways, the helping hands of a community can build a continued bond. Again, this type of exchange is accomplished by some through online communities of various types, including chat rooms or email newsletters. This allows for a group of like-minded individuals to share pictures and stories about their companions.

Sometimes the community is smaller. One parent utilized a scrapbook as a means of recalling the memory of a beloved animal companion for his four-year-old child. Partners shared memories of their dog as means of offering and receiving support to one another. Sometimes, I walk by Kelsey's picture on my shelf and say to Sadie, "Remember Kelsey?" I stand there for a moment, and Sadie's presence helps me recall the bond with my old friend.

A sense of community can be discovered by reading memoirs of those who have also lost an animal companion, and be important for those who might otherwise feel alone in their grief. Hearing stories makes it all right to grieve our own loss by knowing there are others out there who understand and feel the same. In this example, community was created through the efforts of someone only ever met through the pages of a book.

Post-traumatic growth and finding meaning

As already mentioned, sometimes the response to loss involves post-traumatic growth – a positive change – whereby a person grows as a direct result of dealing with grief. Post-traumatic growth is not easy work, as a fundamental aspect of us is altered, and can include having greater capacity for intimacy, more compassion, or assuming new life roles.[22] Some individuals become personally stronger, more connected spiritually, and have a deeper appreciation for various previously-unrealized aspects of life.

When the change is undertaken as a way to connect and remember an animal companion, the growth becomes the foundation for the continuing bond. Many appreciate animal companions for their courage, kindness, or ability to teach lessons not yet fully learned in our life. Some men utilized the post-traumatic growth approach as a way of reprioritizing life, including spending more quality time with other loved ones, both human and animal companions, stating that their dog inspired them to do so. Others try to forgive those who have wronged them, and this includes longstanding anger or resentments toward parents, again, drawing upon the motivation that their canine companion seemed forgiving of their own shortcomings.

There are also those animal companions who must have had a former life either as an arctic explorer or a cruise director, because of their adventuresome spirit and sense of vigor. Dogs such as these specialize in a life of play (and mischief), and draw others into the fun. Calling on the memory of an old friend like this provides the motivation to put down the laptop and engage in life beyond the constraints of our own four walls.

The need to find meaning after loss can occur with an animal companion as well. The new purpose can hit home in a personal way, becoming the basis for how to connect and form a continued bond. The meaning can have to do with the circumstances of first meeting an animal companion, or it can be derived from the scenario leading to their loss. One person remarked about their dog who, having lost one of his four legs to cancer, still maintained a resilient attitude, relearning to walk, even galloping and playing with other dogs. The memory of that dog, and those like him, is the stuff of inspiration, not only for a personal awakening but also to be involved in a mission that helps others.

Likewise, each time I make a small donation to a charity supporting animal companions, it becomes a meaningful way to remember Kelsey. I pause and think for a moment that I met her because of organizations that took in stray dogs. Some similar examples include those who volunteer at local shelters, or are involved in setting up networks to foster abandoned dogs. In one instance, when someone remarked how a rescue volunteer saved dogs from dangerous situations, he candidly replied that dogs were really the ones who saved him. In this case, his own animal companion formed a lifeline, rescuing him from a sense of depression and loneliness.

In some instances, people were prompted to take action to improve local or state laws. They became advocates of social change, improving dog shelter conditions, leading to the betterment of the lives of animal companions. In each of these examples, the presence of the continued bond is felt as we find new personal meaning and purpose in the aftermath of loss.

Psychoanalyst George H Pollack argued that bereavement often concludes through a creative gesture.[23] In the context of helping form various versions of a continuing bond, it can be thought of as a symbolic way of breathing new life into the lost connection. Some may create a foundation or organization that works toward finding a cure for a disease or disorder, or others,

perhaps, discover meaning in a cause that resonates with the life of the lost loved one. It may also take the shape of chronicling our own story, in which people and animal companions cross paths in significant ways. The creative spark embedded within the search can lead to the construction of a personal memorial of pictures, mementos, and the like. In each of these types of searches, a new bond has been established by calling on memories from the past.

Do dog have souls?

James Herriot, author of *All Creatures Great and Small*, tells of an encounter with a penniless Yorkshire widow whose comfort is derived from the company of her animal companions.[24] The widow had been confined to her bed for some time, and above her head hung a cardboard sign on a string that stated, in handwritten letters, "God is near." She asked the young veterinarian making a house call what he thought happened to dogs after they died, "Do they have souls?"

The young vet was not practiced in dealing with these more spiritual matters and tried to skirt the issue in a respectful way. But the widow pressed him, breaking with her usual stoic appearance, tears forming in her eyes. She did not care to be placated and wanted to know his true opinion, regardless of the answer. He paused, then looked straight in her eyes and said, "Wherever you go, your dogs will follow."

Since I was a boy, I have

heard many different versions of the hereafter. Do dogs have souls? How about people? If so, where do they all go? The widow in the story is not the only one deriving comfort from the notion, "Wherever you go, your dogs will follow."

About six weeks or so after her passing, I knew it was time to spread Kelsey's ashes. I could wait no longer. I felt like she was still bound to me. My last duty as a friend was to let her go, but go where I was not sure. I had come to believe that people and dogs move to some type of afterlife. I found relief in stories about how the Buddha was once a canine in one of his many incarnations. I imagined the next world as a staging ground for another try, some downtime before undertaking the next chapter in our existence, in which subsequent lessons are learned. Taking them all in one short lifespan seemed like a task that one never could hope to accomplish. Perhaps there is even the possibility of fellow travelers, someone to share these experiences with in the guise of various companions. Some of these we run into on occasion in different forms, a friend, family member, or even a dog. In the great scheme of things, maybe the temporary masks worn may not matter as much as the connection that is felt. Periodically, our mix of companions may play certain roles in each other's new reality, crossing paths for a few select minutes, days, years, or even, on occasion, a good chunk of a lifespan.

Kelsey's remains came back to me sealed inside a plastic bag, held by a small cardboard box. My first thought was, how could someone who weighed 40-plus pounds be reduced to a few handfuls of ashes? I had been keeping the container in her old ceramic dog bowl with 'Kelsey' etched on the front. A former student in one of my psychology classes gave it to me – how many years ago now? – I was not sure. I just imagine the student heard me make dog parallels to human behavior probably one time too many, and felt sorry for me as a teaching fellow working on my Ph D. It was a nice bowl, better than my dinnerware as a student for sure, and, if push came to shove, I would have eaten out of it.

It was a rainy Sunday morning when I drove to a nearby wooded hiking area for the ceremony. The first time I saw this secluded place at the top of a hill, it struck me that this was where I would bring Kelsey when the time was right. At the busiest time, there was only the occasional car, bike, or jogger. Overall, it was pretty private. I pulled the truck to the side of the road and positioned myself with Kelsey's ashes for the memorial. I was not entirely sure what to say. There was another moment of gratitude as I unzipped the bag and let the ashes fall. Some hit the ground for an instant, and others were immediately carried up by the wind.

Moments of intense sadness often seem poised to be counterbalanced by some act of kindness. Sometimes these events occur with those who are loved, and other times alongside strangers, who may seem to have been recruited unwittingly, becoming a flag bearer for just one moment, which may affect another person in a deep way. These spontaneous gestures arise from within, but I believe they are also prompted on a higher level. It is as if the universe needs to find equilibrium by not allowing things to fall too much to one side. Even for insignificant events such as mine, maybe the culmination of too many unfiltered and grief-filled moments starts to tilt the cosmos a little on its axis. There needs to be a recalibration, even for happenings that may only be recorded by two people.

After I spread Kelsey's ashes, I commended her spirit upward onto the next existence. I tried to picture her in my mind, rising up past the hills in the background, finding her way. I thought to myself, "What will I do without my old friend?"

As I finished, it must have been obvious to the elderly man jogging up the solitary road and past the makeshift memorial service that something heavy was afoot. The man saw me release the ashes and mumble to myself, as I wiped my eyes. He made note of my out-of-place Texas truck tags, and spoke in a kindly voice as he solemnly passed by: "God bless Texas."

This event may seem so small and simple, someone taking just a moment to offer a kind word or two of support. But for me, it stuck. I think back on it now, and maybe it was part of the seed being planted that the sadness I felt did not have to linger, at least not in the way it did. Forming a continuing bond is not meant to be cure-all, but whether or not you subscribe to the notion that, "Wherever you go, your dogs will follow," it acts as a way to keep the dialogue going.

Dog tracks lead home

So many of the aspects involved in search and recovery are familiar to me. I encounter them in my office, and many times while walking with Sadie. I hear stories, heartfelt ones, about companions, large and small. Sometimes they begin with regret, other times humor, and even a sense of nostalgia. If Sadie is present, sometimes, the storyteller unwittingly tries to pet her. In that instant, my canine companion becomes a conduit to someone else's past and a link to their own story. Even in the midst of my own juggle of busyness, I am drawn into the moment. I listen and am often moved. In these encounters, the storyteller's narrative simultaneously also allows me to visit with an old friend of mine.

I shared earlier that Kelsey began to lose her vision in the last months. This was both tragic and ironic, because, in the truest sense, she was witness to my life for the better part of fourteen years. While her eyes are no longer on me, after a long intense search, I can see her now. Not in the sense of some optical illusion, but rather as a part of life that impacts many of my motivations and behaviors. While I have mementos to remind me of our tie, this part is less tangible, though certainly portable, and beyond the reach of decay or despair.

At the heart of all tales involving attachment and loss is how a well-meaning other still has the power to affect how we see the world, others, and ourselves, after passing. I also realize now that our personal story of an animal companion is actually a love story of sorts. As is always true with the great loves of our lives (significant others, children, friends, family, animal companions), there is a genuine power in finding a way to remember; not forget.

For some, the valuing of the human-animal bond might seem to be a recent occurrence. However, based on historical evidence, various animals, like dogs, cats, horses, and cows, have carried a friendly, if not familial, tie in some parts of the world for quite a long time. In some instances, this connection is a venerated one, such as the case with a recent *National Geographic* exposé on mummified dogs and cats in ancient Egypt.[25] The practice dated back to 2950 BC, when lions, donkeys, and dogs were mummified participants in the funeral processions of Egyptian kings and other elite.

However, it was also discovered that the Egyptian masses were sometimes accompanied by animals into the afterlife, such as a man named Hapi-men, who was buried with a small dog at his feet. Egyptologist Salimalkram notes, "Pets, food, death, religion. They cover everything the Egyptians were concerned with." The idea was that animal companions were mummified so that they, too, would join their masters in the afterlife, providing them with companionship. In the end, perhaps just like the ancient Egyptians, when separated, we

also feel compelled to find a way to facilitate a reunion.

The sentiment of my own personal animal companion story mirrors and is interwoven with the accounts of others. True to the rhythm that marks some version of the human-animal bond known and practiced as collective for many thousands of years, an attachment is formed, the core of us is touched, and, when the bond is broken, there is a search. We look for a way to reunite and, in doing so, somehow gather all that has been gained from this connection, preserving it as a part of our life. Perhaps, in our minds, the many tracks, human and animal, created from the excursions of various kinds, begin to blur and merge into one.

Grief experts tell us that grief work is rarely a linear journey, even when presented as such in order to give a coherent version of a story. Part of the self-imposed pressure in writing a book such as this is having all things tied effortlessly together by story's end, but I am not sure that grief really works that way. For every definitive statement that tries to convey a semblance of a neat and tidy experience, there are actually many other ambiguous ones that did not make it onto the page: ones that attest to grief's actual, true convoluted nature.

Grief is a thing reworked over time, revisited with each new major life development. My mind instinctively reached out for Kelsey on the day of my wedding after forty-five years as a bachelor, on special anniversaries we once shared, and, of course, when I take full measure of my life. On each of these occasions, it is like checking in with an old friend, sharing updates, feeling her presence lift me up.

The grief I feel for Kelsey today, if it would be accurate to still call it that, has changed over the years. I have a continued bond with her, though that does not offer a cure-all, some all-encompassing protection from the sadness of her loss. However, the comfort I derive from my new connection with her far outweighs the pain. It has turned into a sweet sorrow. If my eyes begin to water, as they often do when dwelling on certain memories, it is because pure love has turned into a pure grief. My pure love/grief feelings for Kelsey can still overwhelm me, inspire me, and fill me with hope. They remind me at the deepest level that good exists in the world.

Creating a book based on our story was a way to remake our bond, while also simultaneously allowing for a sorting through of grief. But any written account cannot do justice to the process that is still at work within me today. I have never stopped missing Kelsey, and, I suspect, never will. She accompanies me on many of my day-to-day adventures, a silent partner gazing out at me from my inner world. Her presence still affects me, and is one of the many ways I know that where one part of our bond ended, another began.

My biggest surprise, and what I did not bargain for, was how important it was to understand the assorted dog tracks spreading out in so many directions across my life. At first glance, they seem random and crisscrossed, and it is only when I pause that I can decipher the hidden messages they seek to convey. Each of these lasting marks leads home. The one I came from, and the one I always hoped to find.

8

A dog of a different color

As I was writing this book, I encountered a steady stream of stories about love, loss, and preserving the tie that binds. Some were told by friends, and others involved chance encounters with those I met. Unexpected, grief-related anecdotes even began appearing in my classroom during the same courses I had taught for years. The material just seemed to change in pivotal places, with new themes being added. Students would wonder aloud with me, "How do you really remake the bond with another that is gone, but not forgotten?" I even found myself taking on a disproportionate number of clients in my private practice who faced issues of grief and loss.

Looking back now, I realize that these were all attempts, some intentional and others not, to understand more about both endings and new beginnings. In these various encounters, I heard touching stories concerning all types of lost companions, ones who were grieved and still missed. The meaning of love and loss began to press on my awareness from all these different perspectives. I am not sure if I could have turned away from the challenges of sorting through them, even if I had tried.

Part of my response was to reopen my personal journal to the time I spent with Kelsey. I began chronicling most of the stories in this book more than ten years ago. I have since revisited them, recognizing the subtle nuances of my own tale involving human and animal companions crossing paths in significant ways, and then I would add bits here and there. But it also involved digging deeply into my own life, and connecting the dots from the events that shaped my early world: those which made me a likely male candidate for finding the bond.

Men and the bond

The bond has many potential meanings for men. I am convinced that they vary by situation, and are, in some cases, as individual as a man's fingerprint: best friend, confidant, a playful companion who leads us to wildness, a connection that keeps hope afloat amid the ups and downs of life, etc. There are perhaps many more meanings – subtler ones – that some men may feel embarrassed to voice. Without our dogs, some of us might be alone ... literally ... which means that, on one hand, men are fulfilling the masculine mandate to be totally self-sufficient, but at the same time, there is a pitiable quality to such self-imposed isolation.

Our animal companions assume a unique place within a man's relational world, one that is both understated and potentially more encompassing. We look to them to fulfill roles that it seems others cannot, in part because of being hamstrung by restricting ideas of what it means to be a man. It also has to do with the fact that what they have to offer is special enough to transcend even the most dogged, man-made barriers. It is not always the case that human friends, family, and companions fail us, but more likely that man and dog are a natural and easy fit from the onset. Our connection is a respite from the 'normal' 24-7 male constraints.

When other life stresses are added to the already strained condition involving being a man, the result is a cumulative challenge to mental health and well-being. Situation-specific stressors can include a difficult attachment/ loss history, chronic economic strife, lack of social support, being a male with a history of incarceration, or experiencing intense military service in war-torn areas. Taken together, males' lives become a much more complex, nuanced narrative that needs to be understood, and, for many of us, if the right dog comes along, there is hope.

While I think that the challenges of modern-day masculinity and accompanying stresses are present for many men, they have a unique influence for those of us who are middle-aged and beyond. Results from a few studies, including my nationwide survey of male dog owners, suggest that, as males age, they report stronger feelings of attachment to their dogs.[1] Likewise, middle-aged men perceive their animal companions as providing more emotional support. The bond takes on a unique importance as men approach midlife. The timeframe in men's lives is fertile ground for the 'midlife crisis,' an occurrence psychologist Daniel Levinson helped popularize.[2] Levinson found that 80 percent of the men he surveyed in the late 1970s reported experiencing this. Other, more recent, estimates place that number around 10-23 percent.

But even if one does not have a full-blown crisis, being at midlife represents a special time in a man's life. As one approaches middle-age, there is the realization, if not reckoning, of what has been accomplished and what remains undone. Themes can involve striving to achieve various aspects of the American Dream – fame, fortune, and personal fulfillment. However, many of us come face-to-face with the reality that our life is half over and, at the same time, so many dreams are forever out of reach. This can provide a startling wake-up call. When these various perspectives come to some level of awareness, men are faced with the important task of deciding who they are and what the meaning of their lives is. This type of ground-moving experience is even powerful enough to prompt revision of some of the masculine misconceptions I have been addressing in this book, ones which may have previously limited life's experience. While all of this may cause men to turn further inward in moments of introspection, ultimately, the task is really about seeing beyond ourselves.

Psychoanalyst Erik Erikson discussed the life stage challenge at midlife that concerns a sense of "generativity" versus "stagnation."[3] One becomes concerned with, "What has my life's work meant?" and "What is it I leave behind?" This struggle is felt more sharply with age. Generativity refers to 'making your mark' on the world. At first blush, that might sound like the most hollow and ego-driven part of traditional masculinity's self-preoccupation: whoever has the most at the end of the game wins, until, that is, it is framed the way Erikson did.

Generativity is really about caring for others, being creative on their behalf, and making the world a better place. Stagnation, on the other hand, refers to the failure to find a way to contribute. Individuals feeling the heaviness of this type of unproductivity are detached or uninvolved with community, and with society as a whole. The many transitions related to work, love, and even unfulfilled dreams, put these themes into context for a middle-aged man.

A client who was an avid golfer talked about "playing the back nine" of his life, trying to avoid the sand traps and sometimes double-bogeys that were a part of the first half of his trip around life's golf course. Or to borrow from novelist Julian Barnes again, "the sense of accumulation" that can occur when life's frustrations pile up, and either one is unaware or too busy to notice their effects. The accumulation can leave many angry, disenfranchised, and wondering, "Is this all there is? Is numbness the reward I receive for my life's work? Is there no way out at this late stage in the game?"

Some men turn to the bond at midlife, because it represents a 'sure bet;' a connection that can be counted upon. After too many letdowns, the power of that type of pure love cannot be underestimated. However, the bond should not just be seen as a self-serving life preserver, only allowing for more treading water in a bitter sea. If it is accurate that men are, as John Bowlby argued, social animals, hardwired to make and sustain a connection, then many have been missing out on our prime directive. The tie between man and dog can fulfill a deep-seated need to know and be known by at least one other before time runs out. For some, this will provide a sense of meaning in itself; for others, a reliable bond also gives encouragement to explore the world, searching for – and perhaps finding – various types of other personal meanings, all the while being glad that there is someone in our corner.

Given the socialization and stressors many males experience, it becomes clearer to me just how crucial animal companions are in our lives. While we need to comprehend more about how the bond may potentially offset some of the challenges that men experience, the connection can also inadvertently create other issues we are only just beginning to understand. For instance, what are all the elements that make the bond between man and dog seem different, perhaps easier? When males walk, run, and play with their dogs, do they enter into a different sphere of relating; one not easily quantified but certainly emotionally significant? Being with a canine companion offers a clear way of interacting that may be a welcome relief for many men, confused by the nature of other relationship rules and proper protocol with human companions. It may even prompt males to act in a similarly direct manner of healthy connecting, shields down. In either case, having established a meaningful bond with animal companion for upwards of twelve to fourteen years, how does a man adjust to the loss? Does male socialization also prevent men from seeking support from

others at these times; instead, dealing with grief in a more private, introspective way when losing human companions?

Another related situation involves making a new bond after losing an old one. Some research suggests that men may have more difficulty doing this with animal companions.[4] It is also challenging to weigh the potential loss of multiple canine companions over the course of a life time versus the possibility of saying 'no' to their presence in our lives. But, as one man shared with me regarding this dilemma, "Why would you deny yourself their company?" Likewise, Konrad Lorenz once remarked about the impossibility of feeling alone as long as one being is truly glad to see you.[5] For some men, a dog is that welcoming presence.

Given that our bond with animal companions rivals in importance that of a significant other, family member, or best friend, it is essential that men grapple with issues of loss, as well as learn about forming continuing bonds. It takes so much to add a new member to the inner circle of a man's relational world. So much work to break through layers of posturing, defensiveness, and the hope of finding someone real, who will, in turn, set the stage in a way that allows us to be the same.

For those who are slow-warmers to others, or not entirely comfortable with visitors in our personal space, it is difficult to quantify what is taken from our life when this special someone is lost; when, literally an essential force in our life goes missing. And even if we wanted to – and it didn't break the rules for being a man – most of us don't have the option of turning to our vast social network to help balance the loss, but, instead, start over from scratch, knowing the arduous journey that lies ahead.

I am not sure whether there is an easy way to gauge the significance of the bond, but its importance is felt across issues of attachment, loss, and forming a continuing bond. I have no doubt that future research about men and dogs will reveal more nuances about our tie, but you do not have to be a social scientist to know its power, as it is revealed in those stories which *are* told, and the others kept close to the heart. It is important to make peace with our own personal narrative, discerning its meaning and attempting to find a purpose when there was not one before. Sometimes, it helps just to tell our story to someone.

There is another aspect of storytelling I'd like to comment on. As I was writing this book, there were times when I struggled to find the right words to describe what Kelsey and I shared. To recall our adventures was easy; what was most difficult was adding the details of what I felt, and why.

This is not the case with Sadie. Some may explain this as a result of time – years separated each set of stories – but it dawned on me that something else was at play.

It turned out that there was another unexpected gift attached to taking the difficult excursion through attachment, loss, and making a continuing bond: it expanded my vocabulary for life experiences, giving them nuance and subtext. Some of the important happenings from twenty-five years ago, when I first met Kelsey, certainly registered with me when they occurred, but at that time I did not have the ability to capture in much detail what was going on, or how significantly it was affecting me. Instead, essential fine points seemed to slip away, which would have to be recovered later in the re-telling. It would not do justice to those heartfelt encounters by explaining them through the use of generic words such, I felt 'good,' 'loved,' 'happy,' etc.

It is too much of a cliché to suggest that, through loss, we develop a renewed appreciation for life. Instead, I would offer that, these days, when I experience aspects of living, like pure love, or even pure grief, they carry a new level of meaning which is more than words printed on the page, or an abstraction that I skip over when reading because I have no way of relating. Rather, I have discovered new colors, shades of browns, grays, and reds, which I never knew existed. The expanded word choice from which I now draw allows more of life to be felt and understood in the moment. Having the ability to make note of its occurrence also helps me realize that something significant is happening. My own limitations as a writer may not allow the reader to fully appreciate the experience I am trying to describe, but I can say that at least it is there and worth finding, and going there whenever possible, even when it entails emotional cost, has changed my own internal landscape.

While there is a certain universal appeal about deepening

and broadening our emotional depth, the significance of such a happening cannot be underestimated in the often emotionally constricted world of men. We are all travelers in a world that can seem chaotic and unpredictable, and one of the best – and, perhaps, most reassuring – elements of our existence is an honest, trustworthy friend. Recognizing and appreciating these connections when they come into our lives, as well as the ability to manage their loss, is vitally important.

I know that writing this book was therapeutic for me. It helped me organize my thoughts and feelings as I grappled to find a coherent picture of my updated version of love and loss. I felt a force propel me forward through the inevitable setbacks, frustrating moments, and points of confusion. I would not be the same man had I chosen to follow the socialized rules for masculinity that, at best, give a mixed picture of how grief should be observed. This meant I needed to move beyond bristling with defensiveness when pushing and being pushed out of my comfort zone. I had to put my stubbornness aside, and, with it, the fear of letting others see too much.

At some point, I realized that the years spent working on this book were my memorial to Kelsey. Writing this manuscript was part of the way in which I formed a new connection with her. I will be very honest: I needed to find it. A large piece of me would be missing without our bond.

I can imagine a time when I return to my journal again. I may still chronicle some experiences from the past, and follow their trajectory to my life in the present, or perhaps even speculate on days to come. There is also a little more room, space for a few more chapters, about a dog of a different color. Sadie, who was originally going to make cameo appearances in the telling of Kelsey's story, helped me realize that the book was far more than a lament for an old friend. Writing about both my animal companions together changed the direction of the book, because their combined presence in my life literally changed me. Sadie has aged, but is with me still today. While overlapping with Kelsey for just a brief time, Sadie and I have shared our own adventures; others are still waiting to be written.

There is also the nature of new attachments to consider. I recently became a first-time father, and I am deeply touched when I see Sadie hover over little Harris in such a protective way. She positions herself between the baby and strangers till I say it is okay, that he is safe. I recall a time, six weeks after Harris' birth, when he begins to cry, and Sadie becomes noticeably distressed. She moves closer as I hold him in my lap, sniffs inquisitively with her wet nose, and eventually offers a gentle lick to the top of his head before laying down at my feet.

I am deeply touched by Sadie's actions, and I want to offer something, the first truth a father can present his son. At first I try to form my thoughts into a nursery rhythm, but then quickly remind myself that I am not lyrical. Instead, simple words will have to do. I bend down, point in the direction of Sadie, and whisper these words in his newborn ears, "Dogs are special friends."

It hits me then how much older I am than the typical first-time father. I imagine all the experiences Harris will have, and wonder how many I will be fortunate enough to share with him. As though I need to account for these thoughts as well, I add one more verse to the life lesson I want him to hear: "And dogs will be there for you when needed." Maybe, one day, my son will have his own stories to share about his animal friends. Perhaps there will even come a time when little Harris is not so little anymore, and I place him into their gentle care. In either case, the bond forms a distinct part of our family tree, which brings me to the last subject of the book, making new connections while preserving the old ones.

New loves

In the older psychological theories, finding a new loved one is the ultimate end of grieving.[6] It was argued that loving again showed a readiness to move forward with life, and demonstrated that one had healed. After a significant loss, many face the decision about opening ourselves to new relationships. But I do not see it as always a necessity, and nor is it proof positive that the end of bereavement's road has been found. As some individuals have shared with me, their heart feels full enough, after the bond with a loved one has been remade.

For others, there was a choice – and I really mean something undertaken with thoughtful intent – to open up the heart to new opportunities. But even when this was done, it was not always the case that new companions fell into the same category, or fit in the exact same way. Instead, those who desired a new bond sometimes explored different avenues of connection. There could be new types of friends, family members, romantic partners, in some cases, and of course, animal companions. For all these scenarios involving new bonds, prep work is necessary.

Grief experts suggest that our connection with a lost loved one, especially in the instance of a continued bond, prompts us to revisit and revise our tie within the context of fresh life events,[7] which includes the addition of new loved ones. I can attest to how the re-sorting occurs. When I have opened up my heart to another since losing Kelsey, I have felt the need to figure out how all my loved ones belong together now. When I have not rearranged well enough during the waking hours, I sometimes have dreams, where temporary jostling among the key players also occurs.

In the wake of loss, it is also normal to have a mix of feelings about new connections. Initially, the new bond cannot help but be intermingled with, even compared to, the old one(s). This occurrence can lead to some confusion, even sometimes guilt over perceived conflicts of loyalty, as sadness or pining can be reawakened regarding the old tie, even amidst the joy of connecting with a new companion. Hopefully, at some point, a sense of clarity can be obtained that the old and new bonds do not have to be in conflict over the property lines that mark our heart and psyche. Welcoming another into our midst is not a form of disloyalty; nor is it an indication that the lost loved one is now replaced. The challenge is to recognize that the loves of our lives are not built on top of each other, like some old building that must come down in order for a new loft apartment to be erected in its place. Rather, making new bonds while preserving the old ones involves a different type of construction, where the foundations for our various connections are established alongside one another, each in its own appropriate space. In this way, all ties can co-exist peacefully, metaphorically forming a rich neighborhood of significant bonds, rather than one single, overpowering structure, in which all else is swallowed by its shadow. If we are able to successfully grapple with the tasks of attachment, loss, and continuing bonds, then welcoming another into our lives actually helps preserve the old bonds in a special place.

There have been times since her passing when I have visited the bookshelf in my office, the final resting place of the bowl with 'Kelsey' embossed upon it. Instead of dry mix, it now holds pictures, an old collar, and a few other pieces of memorabilia. Seeing and touching these things often brings forth a warm remembrance that the passing years can in no way diminish. Sometimes, caught up in the rush of memories that come to mind, I do not notice, until I turn around, that Sadie has appeared behind me, sitting, staring at me. When this first occurred, I felt awkward, and had a sense of needing to provide an explanation: "Oh, this ... well, uh ... the bookshelf needed dusting ..." Even if I concocted in my mind that Sadie's reaction is a territorial one, a Border Collie's predilection for herding and marking boundaries, I have realized that my two bonds are in no way in any real competition.

While I have already mentioned a number of adventures with Sadie, I have saved two of my favorites for last. This involves the day we met, and then one fall morning, how we met again for the first time.

A new kid on the block

Kelsey was about 12 years old, and I could tell she had lost a step. It struck me one day that maybe a new canine friend would be of help: after all, she fared well with my brother's dogs, her canine cousins up in Kansas. I began working this over in my mind, contemplating getting another dog for Kelsey's sake, a new member of the pack, a new kid on the block. I had heard all the dog folklore about how introducing a pup may stir some activity, even in a senior citizen. Maybe it would be like a Hollywood buddy film, where the old veteran befriends the rookie. They could learn from each other. The old dog gets a new lease of life, and the younger partner benefits from the tutelage. Well, it may not work out that way exactly, but it wouldn't hurt to go take a look.

I went to the Houston SPCA, where I wandered around, and then saw a young Border Collie. She was in a kennel with another dog much bigger than her, but the Border Collie kept making circles around the other, literally herding the larger one in the small space. The big dog looked exhausted from what I am sure was a good cardio workout gone awry. He stared out from the kennel at me, as if to say, "Look, pal, if you don't take me home, at least take her! She is driving me crazy!"

In that moment, I had a rather surreal experience. I began looking at the Border Collie very closely, noticing her markings, her youthful exuberance, and then I heard a woman's voice say in my ear: "Her name is Sadie." I turned to thank her, but no one was there. I turned and turned around again, making sure I didn't miss the person who spoke (which may have looked as if Sadie was herding me as well, this time from inside the kennel!). I am not sure if I was actually me who had lost a step, or if the guardian angel of dogs was dropping a hint, but it worked. I walked up to the kennel and said, "Hi, Sadie. How would you like to meet Kelsey?" There was no clear reply from Sadie, or the now-silent woman, but the other dog who had been running laps, mostly at Sadie's prompting, sure seemed happy.

So I went home and talked it over with Kelsey, and then returned. We went to the play area in the SPCA to see how they would mix. Much to my surprise, they played, sniffed, and Kelsey was showing more energy than usual. Well, that was that, and Sadie came home with us. The rest is history. Sadie was to play a supporting role in Kelsey's life, but also far more in mine.

Then, about a month after Kelsey passed away, I was starting to feel the effects of the medical troubles that would go on for years, and, no doubt, feeling down about losing my best friend. I was at home, sick and lying down. I heard Sadie approach and jump up on the bed, positioning herself right at my side. Before hunkering down she paused and looked right at me, seeming to check if this new arrangement was okay. Kelsey was the self-appointed guardian of the bedroom area, and Sadie made very few visits that weren't greeted by a growl. In some ways, one companion originally had over-shadowed the other, but I was very pleased to have Sadie by my side, which is where she has stayed now for many years.

Once, a long time ago, I had a Lassie-like daydream involving a dog strong enough to save a boy who fell down a well. Instead of a Hollywood creation, I have been lucky enough to have two real canine friends who have helped pull me up to a safer place, and, for this and many more reasons, I am deeply and significantly tied to them both. My recollection of one, while distinctive, keeps the memory of the other intact, accomplished, in part, through the thematic sorting of experiences to which they both belong. Sadie has reaped the benefits and sometimes the challenges of having Kelsey make such an impression on me, but I have learned to see more clearly that significant bonds are never exact replicas; nor must there exist a rivalry between them. All noteworthy connections have their own size, shape, and meaning, and each has the potential to impact our lives. When I acknowledge these facts regarding bonds both old and new, I pay homage to those who went before, as I warmly embrace those in my company now.

While counter to all the messages I learned about being a man when growing up, I realize now that the richness of my existence is derived, in large part, from the bonds that have touched my life. I truly believe a version of my important others exists in my inner world, the place where many of my continued bonds are made. I see them in my mind's eye, I call on their memory, and then we visit together. There is a comfort from their presence. They help me realize, in spite of many years of protest to the contrary, that, at heart, I am a social creature. Even amid my lingering avoidant tendencies, there is more of a want and willingness to make a bond with others, and the tendencies seem to melt away a little easier now because of the influence of my animal friends.

I have also wondered, since writing this book, if the next round of goodbyes will be any different. I know, one day, grief will come again. Sadie is now a few years older than Kelsey when she passed. I try and push that fact to the corner of my mind, but am jolted back to reality when she has a bad mobility day, due to arthritis in her back and hips. I see her hobbling on some days when the weather turns cold, or even, on one occasion, taking a tumble down the stairs. My mind thunders, imagining the worst, "Not yet, Sadie, not yet ..." It is hard to picture my life without her. She has become entwined in the everyday events and the decisions I make – where to live, how I spend each morning and evening on our walks in the woods. Some of my most cherished memories involve a time in my life when I was down and nearly out, and yet Sadie found a way to reach me, when it seemed no one else could.

Among some Native American tribes are stories bordering on legends about the various important roles dogs have played within the community. While canines assumed the practical task of carrying packs, an essential function for a nomadic people accustomed to moving with the seasons, it was also believed that these animal companions possessed a magical nature. Dogs were imbued with the ability to portend good/bad omens, and see into the spirit world where humans could not. However, most remarkable was their ability to absorb and carry the pain, sorrow, and physical troubles of tribe members. The story goes that a dog would bear these aliments to make a human being's load lighter.

I have wondered, at times, whether Sadie possesses some of these magical dog characteristics. She did not carry packs for me when we moved around in and out of state, but, with age, Sadie began developing a lump, which protruded from the ribcage area.

Viewed from the side, it gave her the rather distinguished appearance of having a deep, broad chest. Over time, it took on the look of a Buffalo hump, but on the underside of her torso instead of between her shoulders. While our vet assured me that the lump was not cancerous, and was not causing her any discomfort, at times it constrained Sadie's movement. I have wondered over the years whether Sadie has assumed the role of carrying for me the burden of loss and transition, and if the lump is a physical representation of her care while I was in distress. I think of ways to repay her.

In turn, I would gladly absorb Sadie's physical pain into my own limbs and joints, in order to make her remaining years easier. I would even strike a bargain to take on any of the discomfort of passing, rolling it into my own, if it meant I could ease her eventual journey.

Sometimes, I wish that loss were not a part of loving, though do now have a better sense that Love and Loss are not enemies at war with each other, as I had often felt previously. Instead, they are the most ancient of partners, joined together in an eternal dance. When one set of steps gives way to another, a new round begins, holding the possibility that other actions may also occur. Even if bonds are inevitably broken, there is also the prospect they can be remade. Embedded within each ending is the hope of a new beginning, and I realize, now, that fear should not be at the heart of the love I offer or its subsequent loss, though sometimes it still is.

I see these various insights about attachment, loss, and continued bonds at work in me. I am a different companion (with people and animals), and no doubt a different man because of them. What I have learned compels me forward. Perhaps I have also become a dog of a different color: one whose tracks now move in a new and different way.

Postscript

Dear Kelsey,

I wish you were still here. It has been more than ten years since the last time I saw you. I got the idea to write this letter from a client I saw today. She wrote to her child, who she lost a number of years ago. I think of you as my child, friend, and family. Sometimes, when the memories we shared come back to me, it's like all those roles are wrapped into one. I think that is part of the reason why it has been so hard to lose you. I never really realized how many ways you touched my life till you were gone.

Sadie is all grown up now; in fact, you may not recognize her. She is an old girl with grey streaks, and her teeth have gotten nubby. She likes chewing on treats and bones, just like you did. We walk together every morning and evening … I sold the old house we all lived in; it was too sad to keep living there after you were gone. The new house backs up to the woods, and we see all kinds of animals: deer, wild turkeys, and your favorite, squirrels.

I remember you each year on the day you passed. I go to the park where I spread your ashes. Sometimes as I sit there, I think I can feel you nearby, just like old times. I wonder what you are doing now. Have you moved on to an afterlife or another existence? I sometimes hope that I will bump into you one day on the street or at a dog park, or maybe you will appear as a stray dog who mysteriously shows up at my front door. In either case, I know I would recognize you, no matter what.

Wherever you are, I hope you are happy and well. You deserve it; you brought so much to my life; made it possible for other connections to be made.

I finally got married. My wife is very nice, but she likes the house cleaner than we use to keep it. Remember how the ants would show up from time to time? I also have a little boy. I think you would like him, too. He plays and smiles, and is so full of life. His hair is blonde, like yours. One day I will tell him about you and how you helped me, kept me company, and stayed by my side: all the things a best friend does. I don't think I will ever stop missing you until I see you again.

Chris

Notes

Chapter 1

1 Aristotle. 'Poetics or Poetica.'

2 Normand, C L, Silverman, P R, & Nickman, S L (1996). Bereaved children's changing relationships with the deceased. In Klass, D, Silverman, P R, Nickman, S L (Eds), Continuing bonds New understandings of grief. New York: Taylor & Francis.

3 Cain, A O (1983). A study of pets in the family system. In "New Perspectives on Our Lives with Companion Animals" H Katcher and A M Beck (Eds), pp 72-81, Philadelphia, PA: University of Pennsylvania Press.

Cowles, K V (1985). The death of a pet Human responses to the breaking of the bond. Marriage & Family Review 8, (3-4), 135-148.

Voith, V L (1985). Attachment of people to companion animals. Veterinary Clinics of North America Small Animal Practice, 15, 289-295.

4 Calhoun, L G & Tedeschi, R G (2004). The Foundations of Post-traumatic Growth New Considerations, Psychological Inquiry, 15, (1), 93-102.

Tedeschi, R G, Calhoun L G (2004). Post-traumatic growth Conceptual foundations and empirical evidence. Psychological Inquiry, 15, 1-18.

5 Klass, D, Silverman, P R, Nickman, S L (1996). Continuing bonds New understandings of grief. New York: Taylor & Francis.

6 Kimmel, M (2008) Guyland The Perilous World Where Boys Become Men. New York: Harper Collins.

7 Swann, C The myth of the man-cession. Thomson Reuters, Oct 6, 2009.

8 Brown, S, & I-Fen, L (2012). The Gray Divorce Revolution: Rising Divorce Among Middle-Aged and Older Adults, 1990-2010. Journal of Gerontology Series B, Psychological Sciences Social Sciences, 67, (6), 731-741.

9 O'Neil, J M (2008b) Summarizing 25 years of research on men's gender role conflict using the Gender Role Conflict Scale: new research paradigms and clinical implications, The Counseling Psychologist. 36, 358-445.

O'Neil, J M (2013). Gender-role conflict research thirty years later. An evidenced-based diagnostic schema, Journal of Counseling and Development, 91, 499-498.

O'Neil, J M (2015). Men's Gender Role Conflict: Psychological Costs, Consequences, and an Agenda for Change. Washington, DC. APA Books.

10 "The New American Man Doesn't Look Like His Father." National Public Radio, June 23, 2014.

11 Allen, K, Blascovich, J, & Mendes, W B (2002). Cardiovascular reactivity and the presence of pets, friends, and spouses The truth about cats and dogs. Psychosomatic Medicine, 64, (5), 727-739.

Friedmann, E, Katcher, A H, Lynch, J J, & Thomas, S A (1980). Animal companions and one-year survival of patients after discharge from a coronary care unit. Public Health Reports, 95, (4), 307-312.

Morrison, M L (2007). Health benefits of animal-assisted interventions. Complementary Health Practice Review, 12, (1), 51-62.

Siegel, J (1991). Beneficial effects of pet ownership on some aspects of human health and behaviour. Journal of the Royal Society of Medicine, 84, (12), 717–720.

Serpell, J M (1993). Companion animals In sickness and in health. Journal of Social Issues, 49, (1), 157-167.

Wells, D L (2009). The effects of animals on human health and well-being. Journal of Social Issues, 65, (3), 523-543.

12 The Human Society of The United States statistics, 2012-2013.

13 Australian Companion Animal Council Inc (2010), Contribution of the Pet Industry to the Australian Economy (7th ed).

14 Sendak, M (1963). Where the Wild Things Are. New York: HarperCollins.

Chapter 2

1 Margery Williams (1922). The Velveteen Rabbit or How Toys Become Real. New York: Doubleday & Company.

2 Ainsworth, M D, Blehar, M, Waters, E, & Wall, S (1978). Patterns of Attachment: A Psychological Study of the Strange Situation, Hillsdale, N J Lawrence Erlbaum.

3 Hazan C, Shaver P R (March 1987). "Romantic love conceptualized as an attachment process." Journal Personality & Social Psychology, 52, (3) 511-24.

Bowlby, J (1988). A secure base, New York: Basic Books.

4 Ainsworth, M D S (1982). Attachment Retrospect and prospect. In C M Parkes & J Stevenson-Hinde (Eds), The place of attachment in human behavior (pp 3-30). New York: Basic Books.

Ainsworth, M D S (1989). Attachments beyond infancy. American Psychologist, 44, (4), 709-716.

Ainsworth, M D S, Blehar, M C, Waters, E & Wall, S (1978). Patterns of attachment A psychological study of the strange situation. Hillsdale, NJ: Erlbaum.

Peter Fonagy, Gergely Gyorgy, Elliot L Jurist, Mary Target (2002). Affect Regulation, Mentalization, and the Development of the Self. New York: Other Press.

Main, M (2000). The organized categories of infant, child, and adult attachment

Flexible vs inflexible attention under attachment-related stress. Journal of the American Psychoanalytic Association, 48, (4), 1055-1096.

5 Del Giudice, M (2011). Sex differences in romantic attachment A meta-analysis. Personality and Social Psychology Bulletin, 37, 193-214.

6 Pollack, W (1999). Real Boys Rescuing Our Sons from the Myths of Boyhood. New York: Holt, Henry & Company, Inc.

7 Levant, R F (2001). Desperately seeking language Understanding, assessing and treating normative male alexithymia. In G R Brooks and G Good (Eds). The new handbook of counseling and psychotherapy for men (Vol 1, pp 424-443). San Francisco: Jossey-Bass.

8 Bergman, S (1995). Men's psychological development A relational perspective. In R F Levant & W S Pollack (Eds). The new psychology of men (pp 68-90). New York: Basic Books.

9 Addis, M E & Cohane, G H (Eds), (2005). Social scientific paradigms of masculinity and their implications for research and practice in men's mental health. Journal of Clinical Psychology, 61, 633-647.

10 Wexler, D (2009). Men in Therapy New Approaches for Effective Treatment. New York: Norton.

11 Karen, R (1998). Becoming Attached: First Relationships and How They Shape Our Capacity to Love. New York: Oxford University Press.

12 Melson, G F (2003). Child development and the human-companion animal bond. Animal Behavioral Scientist, 47, 31-39.

13 Nagasawa, M & Ohta, M (2010). The influence of dog ownership in childhood on the sociality of elderly Japanese men. Animal Science Journal, 81, (3), 377-83.

14 Blazina, C & Kogan, L (2016). A New Understanding of Man's Best Friend. New York: Springer.

15 Bonaparte, M (1994). Topsy: The story of a golden-haired chow. New Bunswick: Transaction Publishers.

Bossard, J H S (1944). Mental hygiene of owning a dog. Mental Hygiene, 28, 408-413.

Freud, S (1960). The letters of Sigmund Freud (J S Stern, T, trans). New York: Basic Books.

Levinson, B M (1969). Pet-oriented child psychotherapy. Springfield, Illinois: Charles C Thomas.

Roth, B (2005). Pets and psychoanalysis A clinical contribution. Psychoanalytic Review, 92, 453-457.

16. Ibid.

Chapter 3

1 Lewis, R W B (1959). The American Adam. New York: Phoenix Books.

2 Blazina, C (2001). Analytic psychology and gender role conflict The fragile masculine self. Psychotherapy: Theory, Research, Practice, Training, 38, 50-59.

3 Kimmel, M (2011) Manhood in America: A Cultural History. New York: Oxford.

4 Kimmel, M (2008) Guyland: The Perilous World Where Boys Become Men. New York: HarperCollins.

5 Klein, M (1975) The Writings of Melanie Klein, 4 vols. Hogarth. Vol I: Love, Guilt and Reparation and Other Works, 1921-1945. Reprinted Virago, 1988 (W M K)

Segal, H (1981). The Work of Hanna Segal: A Kleinian Approach to Clinical Practice. New York: Aronson; reprinted Free Association Books/Maresfield Library.
6 Blum, D (2002). Love at Goon Park: Harry Harlow and the Science of Affection. New York: Perseus Publishing.
Harlow, H F, Harlow, M K, Suomi, S J (1971). From thought to therapy: lessons from a primate laboratory. American Scientist. 59, (5), 538-549.
7 Bowlby, J (1979). The making and breaking of affectional bonds. London: Brunner-Routledge.
Bowlby, John (1999). Attachment and Loss: Vol I, 2nd Ed. Basic Books. pp 13-23.
8 Beck, A M, & Katcher, A H (2003). Future Directions in Human-Animal Bond Research. American Behavioral Scientist, 47, (1), 79-93.
Beck, A, & Katcher, A (1996). Between pets and people: The importance of animal companionship. West Lafayette: Purdue University Press.
Friedmann, E, Katcher, A H, Lynch, J J, & Thomas, S A (1980). Animal companions and one-year survival of patients after discharge from a coronary care unit. Public Health Reports, 95, (4), 307-312.
Siegel, J (1991). Beneficial effects of pet ownership on some aspects of human health and behaviour. Journal of the Royal Society of Medicine, 84, (12), 717-720.
Serpell, J M (1993). Companion animals In sickness and in health. Journal of Social Issues, 49, (1), 157-167.
9 Christenfeld, M M R & Nicholas, J S (2005). Dogs still do resemble their owners. Psychological Science, 16, 743-744.
10 Müller, C A, Schmitt, K, Barber, A L A. & Huber, L (2015). Dogs Can Discriminate Emotional Expressions of Human Faces. Current Biology, Mar 2; 25, (5), 601-605.
Marcus, D A, & Bhowmick, A (2013). Survey of Migraine Sufferers with Dogs to Evaluate for Canine Migraine-Alerting Behaviors. The Journal of Alternative and Complementary Medicine, 19, 6, 501-508.
Téglás, E, Gergely, A, Kupán, K, Miklósi, A, Topál, J (2012). Dogs' gaze following is tuned to human communicative signals. Current Biology, 22, (3), 209-212.
11 Derr, Mark (2004). Dog's Best Friend: Annals of the Dog-Human Relationship. Chicago: University of Chicago Press.
Shipman, P (2010). "The animal connection and human evolution." Current Anthropology, 51, 519-538.
Serpell, J, 1989. Pet-keeping and animal domestication: a reappraisal. In: Clutton-Brock (Ed), The Walking Larder: Patterns of Domestication, Pastoralism and Predation. Unwin-Hyman: London.
12 Hortwitz, A (2009). Inside of a dog: What Dogs See, Smell, and Know. New York: Scribner.
13 Kun Guo, Kerstin Meints, Charlotte Hall, Sophie Hall, Daniel Mills (2009). Left gaze bias in humans, rhesus monkeys and domestic dogs. Animal Cognition, 12, (3), 409-418.
14 Stern, D (2000). The Interpersonal World of The Infant: A View from Psychoanalysis and Developmental Psychology. New York: Basic Books.
Winnicott, D (1965). The maturational processes and the facilitating environment: Studies in the theory of emotional development. The International Psycho-Analytical Library, 64, 1-276.

Winnicott, D (1971). Playing and reality. New York: Brunner-Routledge.
15 Kohut, H (1984). How does analysis cure? Chicago: University of Chicago Press.
16 Winnicott, D (1965). The maturational processes and the facilitating environment: Studies in the theory of emotional development. The International Psycho-Analytical Library, 64, 1-276.
Winnicott, D (1971). Playing and reality. New York: Brunner-Routledge.

Chapter 4

1 Turner, J (1996). The Abstract Wild. University of Arizona Press: Arizona.
2 Thoreau, H D (2013). Walden. New York: Empire Books.
Thoreau, H D (2008). Walking. New York: Akasha Classics.
3 Freud, S (1990). Beyond the Pleasure Principle. New York: Norton.
4 Beck, A M, & Katcher, A H (2003). Future Directions in Human-Animal Bond Research. American Behavioral Scientist, 47, (1), 79-93.
5 Ibid.
6 Jung, C G (1981). The Archetypes and The Collective Unconscious. Princeton University Press.
7 Lopez, B H (1979). Of Wolves and Men. New York: Scribner.
8 Freud, S (2003). The Wolfman and Other Cases. New York: Penguin Classics.
9 Levinson, B (1972). Pets and human development. New York: Thomas.
10 Ibid.
11 Huizinga, J (1938/1971). *Homo Ludens* (Playing Man): A Study of the Play-Element in Culture. New York: Beacon Press.
12 Bekoff, M, & Pierce, J (2009). Wild justice: The moral lives of animals. Chicago, IL: University of Chicago Press.
Bekoff, M (2001). Social play behaviour. Cooperation, fairness, trust, and the evolution of morality. Journal of Consciousness Studies, 8, (2), 81-90.
13 Bradshaw, J (2011). Dog Sense: How the New Science of Dog Behavior Can Make You A Better Friend to Your Pet. New York: Basic Books.
14 Brown, S & Vaughan, C (2010). Play: How it Shapes the Brain, Opens the Imagination, and Invigorates the Soul. New York: Avery.
15 Harlinger, M & Blazina, C (2016). Harlinger, M, & Blazina, C (in press). Exploring the role of playfulness with canine companions in coping with stress: How men are impacted by human-animal interaction through calling on a memory of play. In: C Blazina & L Kogan (Eds), Men and Their Dogs: A New Understanding of 'Man's Best Friend.' New York: Springer.
16 Thoreau, H D (2013). Walden. Empire Books: New York.

Chapter 5

1 Niemeyer, R A (2001). The language of loss: Grief therapy as a process of meaning reconstruction. In: R A Niemeyer (Ed), Meaning reconstruction & experience of loss (pp 261-292). Washington, DC: American Psychological Association.
2 Bowlby, J (1979). The making and breaking of affectional bonds. London: Brunner-Routledge.
Bowlby, John (1999). Attachment and Loss: Vol I, 2nd Ed. New York: Basic Books. pp 13–23.

3 Ibid.

4 Ibid.

5 Wells, D L (2009). The effects of animals on human health and well-being. Journal of Social Issues, 65, (3), 523-543.

6 Nagasawa M1, Kikusui T, Onaka T, Ohta M (2009). Dog's gaze at its owner increases owner's urinary oxytocin during social interaction. Hormone Behavior, 55, (3), 434-441.

7 Bowlby, J (1979). The making and breaking of affectional bonds. London: Brunner-Routledge.

Bowlby, John (1999). Attachment and Loss: Vol I, 2nd Ed. New York: Basic Books. pp 13-23.

8 Bonaparte, M (1994). Topsy: The story of a golden-haired chow. New Bunswick: Transaction Publishers.

Freud, S (1960). The letters of Sigmund Freud (J S Stern, T, trans). New York: Basic Books.

Levinson, B M (1969). Pet-oriented child psychotherapy. Springfield, Illinois: Charles C Thomas.

Roth, B (2005). Pets and psychoanalysis A clinical contribution. Psychoanalytic Review, 92, 453-457.

9 (2010). American Pet Products Association poll.

10 Bowlby, J (1979). The making and breaking of affectional bonds. London: Brunner-Routledge.

Bowlby, John (1999). Attachment and Loss Vol I, 2nd Ed. Basic Books. pp 13–23.

11 Kurdek, L A (2008). Pet dogs as attachment figures. Journal of Social and Personal Relationships, 25, (2), 247-266.

12 Kurdek, L A (2009). Pet dogs as attachment figures for adult owners. Journal of Family Psychology, 23, (4), 439-446.

13. Bonaparte, M (1994). Topsy: The story of a golden-haired chow. New Bunswick: Transaction Publishers.

14 Bowlby, J (1999). Attachment and Loss Vol I, 2nd Ed. New York: Basic Books. pp 13-23.

15 Brown, S (2004). The human-animal bond and self-psychology: Toward a new understanding. Society & Animals, 12, (1), 67-86.

Brown, S E (2007). Companion animals as self-objects. Anthrozoos, 20, (4), 329-343.

16 Ibid.

17 Blazina, C, & Bartone, A (2016). Roles of Man's Best Friend in men's lives: Examining the Psychometric Properties of a Measure Assessing Males' Human-Animal Interactions. In C Blazina & L Kogan (Eds), Men and Their Dogs: A New Understanding of 'Man's Best Friend.' New York: Springer.

18 Cain, A O (1983). A study of pets in the family system. In "New Perspectives on Our Lives with Companion Animals" (H Katcher and A M Beck (Eds), pp 72-81. Philadelphia, PA: University of Pennsylvania Press.

Voith, V L (1985). Attachment of people to companion animals. Veterinary Clinics of North America: Small Animal Practice, 15, 289-295.

19 American Veterinary Medical Association's 2012 US Pet Ownership & Demographics Sourcebook.

Chapter 6

1 Doka, K, & Martin, T (2010). Grieving Beyond Gender: Understanding the Ways Men and Women Mourn, Revised Edition. New York: Routledge.

2 Doka, K (1989). Disenfranchised grief: Recognizing hidden sorrow. Lexington, MA: Lexington.

3 Niemeyer, R A (2001). The language of loss: Grief therapy as a process of meaning reconstruction. In R A Niemeyer (Ed), Meaning reconstruction & experience of loss. (pp 261-292). Washington, DC: American Psychological Association.

4 Brown, K (2006). Pastoral Concern in Relation to the Psychological Stress caused by the Death of an Animal Companion. Mental Health, Religion & Culture, 9, 411-422.

Kidd & Kidd, 1985; 1989.

Prato-Previde, E, Fallani, G & Valsecenchi, P (2006). Gender Differences in Owners Interacting with Pet Dogs: An Observational Study. Ethology, 112, (1), pp 64-73.

Ramirez, M 2006. "My Dog's Just Like Me" Dog Ownership as a Gender Display. Symbolic Interaction, 29, (3), 373-391 (2006).

5 Blazina, C & Kogan, L (in press). An Introduction to Men and Their Dogs: A New Understanding of 'Man's Best Friend.' In C Blazina & L Kogan (Eds), Men and Their Dogs A New Understanding of 'Man's Best Friend'. New York: Springer.

6 Kidd, A H, Kidd, R M (1985). Children's attitudes toward their pets – Psychological reports, 57, pp 17-31.

7 Doka, K, & Martin, T (2010). Grieving Beyond Gender: Understanding the Ways Men and Women Mourn, Revised Edition. New York: Routledge.

8 Niemeyer, R A (2001). The language of loss: Grief therapy as a process of meaning reconstruction. In R A Niemeyer (Ed), Meaning reconstruction & experience of loss (pp 261-292). Washington, DC: American Psychological Association.

9 Ibid.

10 Dante Alighieri. The Divine Comedy (The Inferno, The Purgatorio, and The Paradiso).

11 Fairbairn, D (1952). An object relations theory of personality. New York: Basic Books.

12 Barnes, J (2012). The Sense of An Ending. New York: Vintage Books.

Chapter 7

1 Blazina, C (2010). Life After Loss: Psychodynamic Perspectives on a Continuing Bonds Approach with "Pet Companion." In Blazina, C, Boyraz, G, & Shen-Miller, D (Eds). The Psychology of the Human-Animal Bond (pp 203-224). New York: Springer Publishing.

Cain, A O (1983). A study of pets in the family system. In "New Perspectives on Our Lives with Companion Animals" (H Katcher and A M Beck (Eds), pp 72-81, Philadelphia, PA: University of Pennsylvania Press.

2 Endenburg, N (2005). The death of a companion animal and bereavement. In: F H de Jonge & R van den Bos (Eds), The Human-animal relationship: Forever and a day. Assen: Royal Van Gorcum.

3 Fine, A H (2010). Handbook on animal-assisted therapy: Theoretical foundations

and guidelines for practice 3rd ed (pp 17-32). San Diego, CA: Academic Press.

4 Freud, S (1957). Mourning and Melancholia. In: J Strachey (Ed and trans), The standard edition of the complete psychological works of Sigmund Freud (Vol 14, pp 152-170). London: Hogarth Press. (Original work published 1917.)

Freud, S (1959). "Inhibitions, symptoms, and anxiety." In J Strachey (Ed and trans), The standard edition of the complete psychological works of Sigmund Freud (Vol 20, pp 75-175). London: Hogarth Press. (Original work published 1926.)

5 Hagman, G (2001). Beyond decathexis: Toward a new psychoanalytic understanding and treatment of mourning. In R A Neimeyer (Ed), Meaning reconstruction & the experience of loss (pp 13-32). Washington, DC: American Psychological Association.

6 Klass, D, Silverman, P R (1996). Introduction: What is the problem? In Klass, D, Silverman, P R, Nickman, S L (Eds). Continuing bonds: New understandings of grief. New York: Taylor & Francis.

7 Gay, P (1998). Freud: A life for our time. New York: W W Norton & Company.

Jacobs, A (1994). Freud and the interpretation of the wolf-man dream: A dog story? Contemporary Psychoanalysis, 30, 845-854.

Levinson, B M (1969). Pet-oriented child psychotherapy. Springfield, Illinois: Charles C Thomas.

Molnar, M (1996). Of dogs and doggerel. American Imago, 53, (3), 269-280.

Roth, B (2005). Pets and psychoanalysis: A clinical contribution. Psychoanalytic Review, 92, 453-457.

8 Molnar, M (1996). Of dogs and doggerel. American Imago, 53, (3), 269-280.

9 Klass, D, Silverman, P R (1996). Introduction What is the problem? In Klass, D, Silverman, P R, Nickman, S L (Eds). Continuing bonds: New understandings of grief. New York: Taylor & Francis.

10 Klass, D, Silverman, P R, Nickman, S L (Eds) (1996). Continuing bonds: New understandings of grief. New York: Taylor & Francis.

11 Klass, D, Silverman, P R (1996). Introduction: What is the problem? In Klass, D, Silverman, P R, Nickman, S L (Eds). Continuing bonds: New understandings of grief. New York: Taylor & Francis.

12 (2006). McPherson, M, Smith-Lovin, L, & Brashears, M E (Eds), Social Isolation in America: Changes in Core Discussion Networks over Two Decades. American Sociological Review, 71, 358.

13 Way, N (20013). Deep Secrets: Boys' Friendships and the Crisis of Connection. Cambridge: Harvard University Press.

14 Coontz, S (1992). The way we never were: American families and nostalgia trip. New York: Basic Books.

15 Bowlby, J, Parkes, C M (1970). Separation and Loss Within the Family. In: E J Anthony (Ed), The Child in His Family. New York: Wiley.

16 Parkes, C M (Ed) (1970). Seeking and finding a lost object: Evidence from the recent studies of the reaction to bereavement, Society of Science & Medicine, 4, 187-201.

Parkes, C M (2009). Love and loss: The roots of grief and its complications. New York: Routledge.

17 Lorenz, K (1963). On Aggression. New York: Harcourt, Brace and Company.

18 Bekoff, M (2007). The Emotional Lives of Animals: A Leading Scientist Explores

Animal Joy, Sorrow, and Empathy – and Why They Matter. San Francisco: New World Library.

19 Bowlby, J (1999). Attachment and Loss: Vol I, 2nd Ed. New York: Basic Books. pp 13-23.

20 Packman, W, Field, N P, Carmack, B J, & Ronen, R (2011). Continuing bonds and psychosocial adjustment in pet loss. Journal of Loss and Trauma, 16, (4), 341-357.

21 Meyers, B (2002). Disenfranchised grief and loss of an animal companion. In: K J Doka (Ed), Disenfranchised grief: New directions, challenges, and strategies for practice (pp 251-264). Champaign, IL: Research Press.

22 Calhoun, L G & Tedeschi, R G (2004). The Foundations of Post-traumatic Growth: New Considerations, Psychological Inquiry, 15, (1), 93-102.

23 Pollack, G H (1989). The Mourning-Liberation Process. Madison, Conn International Universities Press, Inc.

24 Herriot, J (1972). All Creatures Great and Small. New York: St Martin's Press.

25 Williams, A R (2009). Animals Everlasting: Wrapped in linen and reverently laid to rest, animal mummies hold intriguing clues to life and death in ancient Egypt. National Geographic, Nov.

Chapter 8

1 Bartone, A, & Blazina, C (in press). Exploring how the human-animal bond affects men in a relational way: Attachment, loss, and gender role conflict in middle-aged and young–men. In C Blazina & L Kogan (Eds), Men and Their Dogs: A New Understanding of 'Man's Best Friend.' New York: Springer.

Kurdek, L A (2009). Pet dogs as attachment figures for adult owners. Journal of Family Psychology, 23, (4), 439-446.

2 Levinson, D J, Darrow, C N, Klein, E B & Levinson, M (1978). Seasons of a Man's Life. New York: Random House.

3 Erikson, E H (1959) Identity and the Life Cycle. New York: International Universities Press.

4 Sochos, A, & Bone, A (2012). Attitudes Towards Continuing Bonds, Attachment Vulnerability, and the Moderating Effects of Gender. Journal of Loss and Trauma International Perspectives on Stress & Coping, 17, (3), 260-270.

5 Lorenz, K (1955). Man meets dog. New York: Houghton Mifflin Company.

6 Hagman, G (2001). Beyond decathexis: Toward a new psychoanalytic understanding and treatment of mourning. In R A Neimeyer (Ed), Meaning reconstruction & the experience of loss (pp 13-32). Washington, DC: American Psychological Association.

7 Klass, D, Silverman, P R, Nickman, S L (1996). Continuing bonds: New understandings of grief. New York: Taylor & Francis.

Normand, C L, Silverman, P R & Nickman, S L (1996). Bereaved children's changing relationships with the deceased. In Klass, D, Silverman, P R, Nickman, S L (Eds), Continuing bonds: New understandings of grief. New York: Taylor & Francis.

More great books from Hubble & Hattie!

People tell stories about what they love, including dogs, and this book is a collection of such stories. Some are spooky, some funny, and some engage the mind in the same way that a detective story does.

Starting with a look at the origins of folk tales involving dogs, you'll find facts, history and humour aplenty from all around the world in this fascinating book.

15.2x22.5cm • paperback • £9.99* • 176 pages • 37 b&w drawings • ISBN 9781845848606

Charlie

THE DOG WHO came in from THE WILD

Hubble Hattie

Lisa Tenzin-Dolma
with a Foreword by Marc Bekoff

The heart-warming true story of how one-eyed Charlie went from traumatised feral dog to joyful family member, bonding with the author, her daughter; making new human and canine friends, and eventually overcoming his fears to settle in to his new life.

22X17cm • paperback • £10.99* • 112 pages
• 47 colour images • ISBN 978184584-84-5

Index